Breed Standard
Cocker Span

COLOUR
Various. In self colours no white allowed except on chest.

SIZE
Height approximately: dogs: 39–41 cms (15.5–16 ins); bitches: 38–39 cms (15–15.5 ins). Weight approximately: 12.75–14.5 kgs (28–32 lbs).

TAI
Set on slightly lower than line of back. Must be merry in action and carried level, never cocked up. Previously customarily docked. Docked: Never too short to hide, nor too long to interfere with, the incessant merry action when working. Undocked: Slightly curved, of moderate length, proportionate to size of body giving an overall balanced appearance; ideally not reaching below the hock. Strong at the root and tapering to a fine tip; well feathered in keeping with the coat.

HINDQUARTERS
Wide, well rounded, very muscular. Legs well boned, good bend of stifle, short below hock allowing for plenty of drive.

COAT
Flat, silky in texture, never wiry or wavy, not too profuse and never curly. Well feathered forelegs, body and hindlegs above hocks.

FEET
Firm, thickly padded, cat-like.

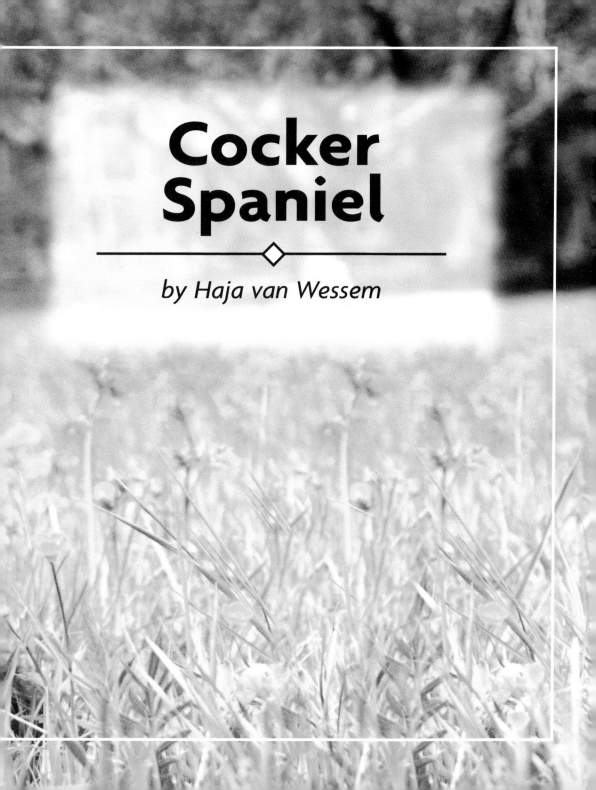

Cocker Spaniel

by Haja van Wessem

9

Table of Contents

27

Origins of the Cocker Spaniel
Trace the ancient beginnings of the Cocker Spaniel as a working gun dog and follow its spread in popularity around the world as a companion dog, show dog, competition dog and ambassador of canine good will.

37

Why the Cocker Spaniel?
Merry, sporting and outgoing: find out about the traits that make the Cocker Spaniel a unique and popular choice for a companion dog. Here are the personality and physical traits of the Cocker as well as breed-specific health concerns.

45

The Breed Standard of the Cocker Spaniel
Learn the requirements of a well-bred Cocker Spaniel by studying the description of the breed set forth in The Kennel Club standard. Both show dogs and pets must possess key characteristics as outlined in the breed standard.

71

Your Cocker Spaniel Puppy
Be advised about choosing a reputable breeder and selecting a healthy, typical Cocker puppy. Understand the responsibilities of ownership, including home preparation, acclimatization, the vet and prevention of common puppy problems.

DISTRIBUTED BY:

INTERPET
PUBLISHING

Vincent Lane, Dorking
Surrey RH4 3YX England

ISBN 13: 978 0966859270
ISBN 10: 0966859278

Copyright © 1999, 2009
Kennel Club Books®
A Division of BowTie, Inc.
Printed in South Korea

Everyday Care of Your Cocker Spaniel
Enter into a sensible discussion of dietary and feeding considerations, exercise, grooming, travelling and identification of your dog. This chapter discusses Cocker care for all stages of development.

87

Training Your Cocker Spaniel
by Charlotte Schwartz
Be informed about the importance of training your Cocker Spaniel, from the basics of house-training, and understanding the development of a young dog, to executing obedience commands (sit, stay, down, etc.).

Photo Credits:
Norvia Behling
Carolina Biological Supply
Doskocil
Isabelle Francais
James Hayden-Yoav
James R. Hayden, RBP
Carol Ann Johnson
Dwight R. Kuhn

Dr. Dennis Kunkel
Mikki Pet Products
Phototake
Jean Claude Revy
Haja van Wessem
C. James Webb
Derek Whitehouse

Illustrations by Renée Low

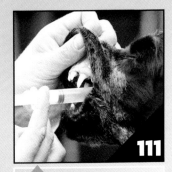

111

Health Care of Your Cocker Spaniel
Discover how to select a proper veterinary surgeon and care for your dog at all stages of life. Topics include vaccination scheduling, skin problems, dealing with external and internal parasites and the medical conditions common to the breed.

139

Your Senior Cocker Spaniel
Recognise the signs of an ageing dog, both behavioural and medical; implement a senior-care programme with your veterinary surgeon and become comfortable with making the final decisions and arrangements for your senior Cocker Spaniel.

145

Showing Your Cocker Spaniel
Experience the dog show world, including different types of shows and the making up of a champion. Go beyond the conformation ring to working trials, gun dog trials, field and agility trials, etc.

157

Understanding Your Dog's Behaviour
Learn to recognise and handle common behavioural problems in your Cocker Spaniel, including aggression with people and other dogs, chewing, barking, mounting, digging, jumping up, etc.

Glossary: **172**
Index: **174**

It is believed that the spaniels, as a general dog type, were identified more than 2,500 years ago. The name derives from the Carthaginian word for rabbit, which is *span*; thus the words *Spain* and *Hispania* also came into usage.

Ancestry of the Cocker Spaniel

EARLY SPANIEL HISTORY

In 500 B.C. when the Carthaginians landed in Spain during one of their travels in the Mediterranean, the soldiers saw a great number of rabbits and they shouted 'Span, span!' (span being the Carthaginian word for rabbit). Thus, the land was called Hispania, or 'rabbit-land,' and the dogs that they saw in pursuit of the rabbits became known as spaniels or 'rabbit-dogs.'

Is this how spaniels got their name? Or is it the fantasy of Virginia Woolf, who tells us this delightful little story in her book *Flush*, the biography of Elizabeth Browning's spaniel. It is very likely that the spaniel lived in the countries surrounding the Mediterranean and thus also in Spain. He might have gotten his name through the Basque word 'Espana;' the fact that there are several spaniel-like breeds in France which are called 'epagneuls' also points in this direction.

The fact is that the spaniel can be considered to be one of the oldest breeds in history. In the Metropolitan Museum in New York a small statue in terracotta can be seen that has a decidedly spaniel-like appearance. The statue is over 2000 years old and belongs to the Cypriote Collection.

More proof of the antiquity of the breed can be seen from the first mention of a spaniel in the Irish Laws in 17 A.D. in a statement that Water Spaniels had been given as a tribute to the King. Spaniels also travelled to

A 2,000-year-old terracotta (clay) figure of an early spaniel-type dog. Most breed historians rely on ancient artifacts to substantiate the relative antiquity of a type of dog.

9

Wales, where they were the treasured dogs of King Howell Dha (Howell the Good). The King's love for his spaniels went as far as giving them a special mention in one of the laws of the country in 948 A.D. At this time, for the price of one spaniel, one could buy a number of goats, women, slaves or geese! In these laws, mammals are divided into birds, beasts and dogs, and the 'dogs' classification was subdivided into tracker, greyhound and spaniel.

The first mention of a spaniel in English literature comes as early as Chaucer (1340–1400) and Gaston the Foix, who died in 1391. Chaucer, author of the *Canterbury Tales*, refers to the spaniel several times ('for as a

DID YOU KNOW?
It was only in the nineteenth century that humans really took notice of the dogs around them: how they looked, what colour they were and how tall they were. Dogs all along have been helpmates—some dogs killed vermin and some dogs protected the property. Breeding a certain dog to a certain bitch was not necessarily accidental. More than likely, humans paired dogs for their abilities. To produce a dog for a specific purpose, they would mate two dogs with the qualities needed for that purpose. Thus were progenerated various dogs with superior abilities.

Spaynel she wol on him lepe'), which proves beyond doubt that the spaniel was known in England 600 years ago. Gaston de Foix mentions the spaniel in his work *Miroir de Phoebus* or, as it is also known, *Livre de Chasse*. Gaston de Foix was a feudal baron who lived in France near the Spanish border, and he was convinced that Spain was the country of origin of the spaniel. 'Another manner of hound there is, called hounds for the hawk, and Spaniels, for their kind came from Spain, notwithstanding that there be many in other countries. Such hounds have many good customs and evil. Also a fair hound for the hawk should have a great head, a great body, and be of fair hue, white or tawny (i.e., pied, speckled, or mottled), for they be fairest and of such hue they be commonly the best.' He then describes them as being 'hounds (the word dog was not used then) with a great head and a great, strong body. Their colour is red and white of orange roan, but black and white can also be seen. They run and wag their tail and raise or start fowl and wild beasts. Their right craft is the partridge and the quail. They can also be taught to take partridge and quail with the net and they love to swim.'

Another early reference to 'Spanyellys' occurs in the *Boke of St. Albans* (1486), also named *The Book of Field Sports*, written by

Dame Juliana Berners, prioress of Sopwell Nunnery, Hertfordshire. It is obviously a school book and it is assumed that the book was written for the use of King Henry IV's son, Prince Henry, to teach him to read and make him acquainted with the names of the animals and phrases used in venery and field sports.

In the book there is frequent mention of spaniels in the royal household. Thus we read that 'Robin, the King's Majesty's Spaniel Keeper' was paid a certain sum for 'hair cloth to rub the Spaniels with.'

NETTING

In the days of Henry VIII, the many banquets called for large amounts of food, of which game was an important part. Game such as partridge, quail, pheasant, rabbit and hare was caught in snares, but because of the never-ending demand, a more speedy method of catching the game was sought. This method was found in 'netting.' Spaniels were used to drive the birds towards the fowlers, who stood ready with their extended nets. Dog and bird were caught under the net. The spaniels that were used for this kind of work were called 'sitting' or 'setting' spaniels, and they are the ancestors of our modern setters.

In his book *Treatise of Englishe Dogges* (1570) Dr. Caius

The word dog is from the Old English 'dogge.'

(pseudonym for John Keyes) described the way the dogs are taught to let themselves be caught under the net. Dr. Caius classified all sporting dogs under two headings: *Venatici*, used for the purpose of hunting beasts, and *Auscupatorii*, used for the hunting of fowl. He subdivided this latter group into 'Setters which findeth game on the land' and 'Spaniells which findeth game on the water.' He named this group

DID YOU KNOW?
Since dogs have been inbred for centuries, their physical and mental characteristics are constantly being changed to suit man's desires for hunting, retrieving, scenting, guarding and warming their masters' laps. During the past 150 years, dogs have been judged according to physical characteristics as well as functional abilities. Few breeds can boast a genuine balance between physique, working ability and temperament.

Hispaniolus. He also was of the opinion that these dogs originated in Spain. He describes them as white with red markings and—be it more rare—red or black, and he gives a special mention to a dog, brought in from France in 1570,

that was 'speckled all over with white and black, which mingled colour incline to a marble blue which beautifieth their skins and affordeth a seemly show of comliness.' That, undoubtedly, was the first blue-roan spaniel!

In the 16th and 17th centuries another group of spaniels was recognised: the Toy Spaniel. Since the Toy Spaniel in those days was bigger and heavier in build than our modern Toy Spaniels, it is very likely that there was a relationship between the Blenheim Spaniel and the King Charles Spaniel and the hunting spaniels. Moreover, it wasn't unusual for Blenheim Spaniels to be used in the field.

The English Springer Spaniel, shown here, exists today as a totally separate breed from the Cocker Spaniel, though both breeds share common ancestors.

THE FIRST COCKERS

With the invention of the gun, netting disappeared and the game was caught by shooting. The setting spaniels were used to find the game and point it so that it could be shot, and the springing spaniels had to flush the game from the cover.

In the *Sportsman's Cabinet,* written by Nicolas Cox and published in 1803, we find a description of the spaniel: 'The race of dogs passing under the denomination of spaniels are of two kinds, one of which is considerably larger than the other, and are known by the appellation of the springing spaniel—as applicable to every kind of game in every country: the smaller is called the cocker or cocking spaniel, as being more adapted to covert and woodcock shooting, to which they are more particularly appropriated and by nature seem designed.' We may assume, therefore, that the Cocker Spaniel derives his name from the woodcock or, as some believe, the cock pheasant. Cox continues to give a description of the Cocker who 'has a shorter, more compact form, a rounder head, shorter nose, ears long (and the longer the more admired), the limbs short and strong, the coat more inclined to curl than the springers, is longer, particularly on the tail, which is generally truncated; colour liver and white, red, red and white,

black and white, all liver colour, and not infrequently black with tanned legs and muzzle.' From the great similitude between some of these Cockers and the small water-dog, both in figure and disposition, there is little doubt but they may have been originally produced by a cross between the springing spaniel and the latter. The Cocker is, again, praised for his rapid action in the field, his tireless enthusiasm in finding and pursuing a hare or in searching winged game. His tail is

Ch. Wribbenenhall Waiter, a turn-of-the-century champion Field Spaniel, was considered an excellent example of the correct Field Spaniel in those days. Excessively long and low dogs were out of fashion because they were inferior workers in the field.

mentioned as 'being in perpetual motion,' a feature that, fortunately, has been preserved in our modern Cockers with their ever-wagging tails.

In the course of the 19th century we see a new variety of spaniel: the Field Spaniel. The main difference between the Field and the Cocker is their weight. The Field Spaniel was a strong, black dog whose weight should exceed 25 lbs.; otherwise, he would be classified as a Cocker.

13

The fact that pups from one litter could be classified as either a Cocker or a Field was detrimental to both breeds and, where the popularity of the Field Spaniel was increasing all the time, the future of the Cocker didn't look too good. The decision of The Kennel Club to recognise them both as different breeds probably

Ted Obo and Tim Obo are still to be found in the pedigrees of our modern Cockers. It was also Mr. James Farrow who, in 1902, founded the Cocker Spaniel Club of Great Britain, which is still going strong today. Also in 1902, The Kennel Club issued the first official breed standard.

A contemporary of Mr.

Fred and Ch. Obo, born in June 1879, were bred by Mr. James Farrow, who built the foundations for the Cocker Spaniel.

saved the Cocker from extinction. Fields and Cockers were both seen at shows and the Cocker began to make steady progress.

HISTORY OF THE BREED IN GREAT BRITAIN

It was undoubtedly Mr. James Farrow who built the foundation for the breed as we know it today. The original Obo was born on June 14, 1879. His Bob Obo was the forerunner of the modern Cocker Spaniel. Names such as Champion

Farrow was Mr. C.A. Phillips, originator of the Rivington strain. He bred black and coloured Cockers that all came from Obo stock. Mr. Phillips had a particular interest in the working side of Cockers and he helped promote the field trials in the beginning of this century. He himself was a very successful competitor and he bred many field trial champions, of whom Rivington Simon, Rivington Rogue and Rivington Reine are

Field Trial Champion Rivington Sam, born in 1911, bred by Mr. C. A. Phillips, shown in a painting by R. Ward Binks.

probably the best known.

In 1875 Mr. R. Lloyd founded his 'Of Ware' strain that later proved to be so incredibly influential. The name 'Of Ware' was not introduced by Mr. R. Lloyd but by his son, H.S. Lloyd, who carried on the kennel after the death of his father. Famous 'Of Wares' were the champions Invader of Ware, Whoopee of Ware and Exquisite of Ware, to be followed by many, many others in later years. The influence of Mr. Lloyds's dogs remained strong until long after World War II.

Another kennel that must be mentioned because of its success and its influence on the history of the breed is the 'Bowdler' kennel of Mr. R. de C. Peele, founded in 1898. Ch. Ben Bowdler was the sire of Ch. Bob Bowdler ex Judy Bowdler, who was also the dam of Ch. Rufus Bowdler. From Jetsam Bowdler and Jock Bowdler came Rocklyn Magic, a dog that is featured in so many pedigrees and who was a very good producer.

Breaside Bustle is a name that is familiar to many of us. He was born in 1894 and was the

You cannot stop a Cocker Spaniel from having fun and performing his inborn retrieving instinct.

Luckystar of Ware, a blue roan, was the Supreme Champion of Crufts in 1930 and 1931. This dog was considered by many to have been the greatest of all Cockers in his day.

Breaside Bustler, sire of such champions as Ben Bowdler and Blue Peter, both great names from the past in the Cocker breed.

Rocklyn Magic, who features in so many influential pedigrees, was a top producer.

sire of Blue Peter, a dog that had a remarkable influence in fixing and transmitting the characteristics of the coloured variety. Another son of Breaside Bustle was Ch. Ben Bowdler. Most of our coloured Cockers trace back to this wonderful sire, Breaside Bustle. Owner of the Breaside Cockers was Mr. J.M. Porter.

During the first World War (1914–1918) all breeding activities stopped, but after the war a few dedicated breeders succeed-

ed in restoring the breed and the Cocker became more popular than ever in the field as well as in the show ring. The conditions in the field, however, changed and the Cockers were asked to retrieve. To be able to retrieve a dog must be in balance, and balance requires a strong neck and a short back. For the longcast, low-legged Cocker with a comparatively short neck, this

new task proved to be impossible and breeders began to aim for a more square, leggier and shorter-backed dog. It was this variety that travelled around the world—Europe, India, South Africa, Australia, China, Canada and New Zealand.

Influential breeders of the period between 1918 and 1940 were Mrs. A.H. Gold of 'Oxshotts,' whose homebred Ch. Oxshott Marxedes was a famous sire; Mrs. Judy de Casembroot of 'Treetops,' who succeeded in establishing a line of very successful and very homoge-

Sixshot Black Swan is said to have been of extreme influence to the solid Cockers of today.

The 'Broomleaf' Kennel, founded by Mrs. Kay Doxford, was to become a powerful force for good red and black Cockers. Her Ch. Broomleaf Bonny Lad of Shillwater not only won 15 Challenge Certificates but he also

A modern Cocker looks quite different than the earlier specimens of the breed.

Until 1902 puppies from one litter could either be a Field Spaniel or a Cocker Spaniel, depending on their weight. The bitch shown here is Madame d'Albany. She is low and long, not at all like the present-day Cocker or Field Spaniels.

neous blacks, of which Treetops Walkie Talkie is probably best remembered; and Mrs. Veronica Lucas-Lucas, who established her 'Sixshots' in the 1930's, starting with blacks and reds but later also including parti-colours.

qualified in the field and proved to be a very good stud dog.

In those years between the two wars the Cockers did extremely well. The breed was popular and flourishing, culminating with the Best in Show wins of Sh. Ch. Lucky Star of Ware at the 1930 and 1931 Crufts Dog Shows. This success was repeated in 1938 and 1939 by Sh. Ch. Exquisite Model of Ware and again in 1948 and 1950 (there was no Crufts in 1949) when Sh. Ch. Tracy Witch of Ware became Supreme Best in Show at Crufts.

Together with Lorna Countess Howe, Mr. Lloyd is the only one to succeed in winning a Best in

A famous Cocker, featured in many of the pedigrees of champion dogs, is Ch. Oxshott Marxedes, bred by Mrs. A. H. Gold.

The famed Broomleaf Kennels, founded by Mrs. Kay Doxford, produced some wonderful dogs as exemplified by Ch. Broomleaf Bonny Lad of Shillwater.

Mr. H. S. Lloyd's incredible success culminated in winning the Supreme Best in Show six times: In 1930 and 1931 with Sh. Ch. Lucky Star of Ware; in 1938 and 1930 with Sh. Ch. Exquisite Model of Ware (shown here); and in 1940 and 1950 with Sh. Ch. Tracey Witch of Ware.

18

Show twice in a row at Crufts—and he did it three times! No breeder since has been so successful. In 1970 Mrs. Joyce Caddy came close when her Ch. Ouaine Chieftain won Reserve Best in Show, and in 1996 Mrs. Patricia Bentley's Caniou Cambrai won Best in Show.

The Second World War (1940–1945) again put a stop to all breeding and many breeders had their entire stock put down, out of fear of the invasion. Whereas during the 1914–1918 war shows continued, this was not the case in World War II. At the end of the war breeders tentatively started to breed again and as the demand for puppies grew, more breeding was undertaken. Mr. H.S. Lloyd still carried on and although he had a smaller number of dogs, he still had a small team of stud dogs on which breeders greatly relied.

New people came into the breed, such as Mrs. Kay Holmes of the 'Pentavy' prefix, who succeeded in establishing herself as a successful breeder and show judge, and Mrs. Sylvia Jones of 'Courtdale,' whose Sh. Ch. Courtdale Flag Lieutenant was a proven sire. His son, Courtdale Sub Lieutenant was exported to Germany, where he contributed greatly in establishing the particoloured Cocker.

A new star, rising very fast, was the 'Lochranza' kennel of Miss Macmillan and Miss Charles. Dogs from their breeding that will always be remembered are Sh. Ch. Lochranza Dancing Master,

In 1996 Sh.Ch. Caniou Cambrai was Supreme Best in Show at Crufts. The dog was bred by Mrs. Patricia Bentley.

Lochranza Merryleaf Eiger, Sh. Ch. Lochranza Strollaway and many, many others.

Having arrived in the 1950s, we find that this decade can be qualified as the vintage for Cocker Spaniels. Many of the old established kennels continued to bring out dogs and bitches of great quality, and kennels that had started during or after the war

became big names in their own right. One of those pre-war kennels that built up strongly after 1948 was the 'Colinwood' kennel of Mr. A.W. Collins. In nearly every pedigree of our modern Cockers we can find the tri-colour 'Ch. Colinwood Cowboy,' who had a tremendous influence on the breed, as well as Sh. Ch. Colinwood Silver Lariot.

Mr. Alf Collins died in the 1960s after having been in the breed for about 40 years. He left the kennels and the prefix to his daughter, Mrs. Woolf, who had been as keenly involved in the Colinwood Cockers as he was and who is still active as a breeder and a judge today.

The 'Craigleith' Cockers, founded by Mrs. Mollie Robinson, are worth a mention. She produced some of the top winners, not only in Great Britain but also in many other countries, notably the United States and South Africa. Her most famous Cockers are probably Sh. Ch. Craigleith Cinderella, Sh. Ch. Craigleith Maggie May, Sh. Ch. Craigleith Sweet Charity and Sh. Ch. Craigleith The Waltz Dream.

In 1963 the Cocker Spaniel world suffered a great loss with

the death of Mr. H. S. Lloyd, but fortunately his daughter, Jennifer, who shared his love for Cockers, carries on with the 'Of Ware' and 'Falconers' prefixes.

The first dog to be registered with the 'Scolys' prefix was Scolys Simon in 1955, bred by Mrs. Dilys Schofield. She bred several champions, at home and overseas, but her most famous one is Sh. Ch. Scolys Starduster, who not only was considered to be the prototype for the standard but who also was a great sire of winners. He is by another dog that turned out to be very influential, Sh. Ch. Goldenfields Minstrel Boy.

Nowadays the breed is still prospering. There are a great number of dedicated breeders and at the shows we see many Cockers of great quality.

THE COCKER ON THE CONTINENT
The history of the spaniel originates on the Continent (in Spain) and throughout Europe we see that every country has its own kind of 'spaniel.' France has the Epagneul, Germany the Wachtelhund and Holland the Kooikerhondje. The first Cocker Spaniels were imported from Great Britain as early as the 1890s. In the first two

decades of this century they were mainly used for hunting and field trials but in the 1920s and 1930s more Cockers were seen on the show benches. Real popularity

Superior quality Cockers are becoming more numerous every year.

only came in the 1930s, but World War II put an end to all breeding. Breeders managed to pick up quickly after the war and in the 1950s and 1960s the breed was flourishing again.

A breeder with an influence that went far beyond the Dutch borders was Mrs. L. van Herwaarden of the 'Wagtail' prefix. She was very determined

There were many beautiful Lochranza Cockers but Sh. Ch. Lochranza Strollaway was undoubtedly one of the best.

Winner of the World Show in Frankfurt, Germany in 1935 was Woodcock's Memory, a Cocker shown by Mrs. L. van Herwaarden of Holland.

Ch. Obo II, founder of the Cocker Spaniel lineage in the United States. Although he looks long and low by modern-day standards, he was considered more functional in type than his forebears. He was bred to no fewer than 72 bitches in the U.S. and Canada.

to establish a good strain of solid and parti-coloured Cockers and managed to import beautiful dogs of excellent breeding from England. For nearly three decades she dominated in the show ring. She exported to most European countries and to the States. Her dogs won numerous Bests in Show in many European countries, but the best known is probably Woodcock's Memory's Best in Show win at the World Show in Frankfurt in 1935.

Nowadays we see a great number of breeders in the various continental countries and at the shows there are always a good number of Cockers, solids as well as parti-colours.

THE COCKER IN AMERICA

The history of the Cocker Spaniel in America is a very interesting one. Few Americans are aware that from the worldwide perspective, the well-known Cocker Spaniel is the English variety. Outside the United States there are Cocker Spaniels and American Cocker Spaniels, whereas in the United States there are Cocker Spaniels and English Cocker Spaniels!

In the 1870s there were quite a number of breeders of Field Spaniels and Cocker Spaniels and, as in England, the dividing line between the two breeds was the weight. The Cocker limit was around 28 pounds, anything above that was a Field Spaniel. This situation changed when in 1884 a couple of Obo sons arrived in utero from England. Mr. Farrow had sent the bitch, Chloe II, in whelp by Ch. Obo, over to Mr. F.F. Fletcher. One of these puppies, Obo II, was sold

to Mr. J.P. Wiley and this dog proved to be as prepotent as his famous sire. What Obo II did for the breed in the States was as important as what his sire Obo did in England—they managed to establish weight and type in the breed. Interest in the breed in the 1890s became very keen and the breed thrived.

However, gradually it appeared that the Cockers were

becoming smaller in size and that some of them looked more like toys. The new standard, published in 1901, did nothing to help that situation—it accepted the Cockers as they were and it did not encourage the development of a stronger, more workmanlike type of dog. Mr. Wiley, whose kennel had been so important in the first years, tried to cross with Field Spaniels. When that did not give him the results he wanted, he eventually retired much to the regret of all Cocker fanciers.

Obviously, something had to be done. The tendency toward a decrease in size, the domed skulls and the round eyes were clearly an inheritance of the King Charles Spaniel blood, introduced at an earlier period. The Cocker became so refined and beautiful that its classification in the Sporting Group was largely a matter of toleration and was being frequently questioned.

However, we have to thank the Sporting Spaniel Society for saving the Cocker from becoming a toy dog and the Springer Spaniel from becoming extinct. These breeders set out, with the material they had—the liver-and-white and black-and-white Keeper's Spaniels, the Clumbers, the old English Water Spaniel, the Sussex and the setter/spaniel crosses that were owned by sportsmen—to develop the

Springer Spaniel. With this breeding they created, as a by-product, a Cocker that was as closely related to the modern Springer as the original Cocker was related to the Field Spaniel.

Mepals Rosemary was an early American Cocker Spaniel.

This could well be the explanation of why so many pedigrees of English Cockers cannot be traced back to Obo II, whereas so many pedigrees of American Cockers can.

Around 1910 the breeders realised that the two types, the English and the American, were no longer compatible and importing had all but stopped. At that time, however, England had developed the more modern English Cocker, the shorter-backed, leggier version, and in the late 1920s these Cockers began to appear in the United States in increasing numbers. This dog, being so different from what the American Cocker fanciers considered ideal, could not compete in the show ring with the Americans, and attempts to incorporate its qualities in the well-established

Geraldine Rockefeller Dodge proved that the English Cocker was a different breed from the American Cocker Spaniel. She wrote a book on the history of the Cocker Spaniel in America to convince the American Kennel Club that the English and American Cocker were two separate breeds. In 1946 the two breeds were officially separated.

The modern American Cocker Spaniel has become quite popular in England. The American breed is larger than the English and requires more grooming expertise to achieve the desired sculptured appearance.

American Cocker were met with unwillingness.

It was thanks to Mr. E. Shippen Willing, a dedicated fancier of the British type, and Mr. Russell H. Johnson Jr., President of the American Kennel Club, that this British type was recognised by the American Kennel Club and was given classes at the shows in 1936. From that moment on, the Cocker Spaniel developed rapidly. Quality Cockers from Great Britain, Holland and Germany were imported and the breed started to establish itself in its own right until World War II put an end to that. Imports stopped, breeding slowed down, dog showing decreased. Mrs. Geraldine R. Dodge, one of the earliest fanciers of the breed, used this relatively quiet period of time to prove that the two varieties were actually separate breeds. She proved that they had been bred separately for more than the five generations required and she rewrote the standard for the English-type Cocker, making it sufficiently different from the standard for the American breed so that there might be less confusion. She succeeded in 1946 when the two breeds were officially separated and the American Kennel Club recognised the English Cocker Spaniel as a breed. While American Cockers remain one of the most popular breeds in the United States, the English Cocker is now also firmly established there.

A beautiful
Cocker Spaniel
produced
in the U.S.

Why the Cocker Spaniel?

COCKER PERSONALITY

If we look at the standard the first words that strike us are 'merry, sturdy and sporting.' That is the essence of a Cocker Spaniel, and the fact that the standard opens with these words may well indicate their importance. A Cocker Spaniel is a happy dog—happy with you and with the family, but also with complete strangers and other dogs. He is happy to work and happy to play; he is the ultimate optimist. He gets up every morning with the joyful expectation of another lovely day, with lots of fun, hopefully a lot to eat (because he loves his food!) and who knows what new and exciting adventures! He will follow you around in the house; he wants to know what you are doing and he would hate to miss some of the fun and excitement. He loves to share his happiness with everybody and if this means that he jumps up on you with four muddy paws, then you have to accept that in the sense with which it was done! His happy, easy-going temperament also makes him a fatalist. If he cannot come with you he will express his great sorrow (and he can look very sorrowful!), but he will accept the situation and make the best of it. If his feet are to be trimmed he will try to wriggle out of it, but if you are firm he will give a mental

A good Cocker should be merry, sturdy and sporting. Above all, it must be a happy dog.

FACING PAGE: Cocker Spaniels are emotional and expressive. First and foremost these are merry dogs that desire to be by your side. Look into this Cocker's eyes to understand why we call the Cocker a 'fatalist.'

27

Temperament in the Cocker Spaniel is the first concern of every breeder. Whether selling a puppy for show or companion only, a Cocker must be sweet and reliable.

problem has mainly occurred in solids. It is of the utmost importance that you buy a puppy from a breeder with a good reputation and preferably one whose dogs you have met. If you know that temperament problems have occurred more than once in a certain line, you would do well to avoid this line.

Although a Cocker thinks that every guest to your house has been invited especially to please him and will therefore be loved by him, he is very loyal and affectionate to his own people. He not only shares your house, he also shares your life, your joys and your sorrow, and he has a special antenna for your moods. The bond between you and your Cocker can become incredibly strong to the point that no words are needed.

Another quality of the Cocker that receives special mention in the standard is his sporting, sturdy, active and lively nature. You must be prepared to give your Cocker, when he has matured, at least an hour of free exercise every day. He will enjoy a walk through the park on the lead, or even a shopping expedition, but he needs more. He needs to have the opportunity to stretch his legs, run at full speed and be able to pick up exciting smells that appeal to his gundog instinct. Woods, fields, dunes, he loves it all...and especially water. If the

shrug and go to sleep on the trimming table. However, this behaviour makes it very important that you are gentle but firm with him because he is clever enough to realise that when he gets his way once, he may get it again, and again...

Sometimes we come across a Cocker with a bad temperament. It should be the duty of breeders not to breed from or use a Cocker with either an aggressive or a nervous temperament. Unfortunately, this does not always happen and it is the unfortunate puppy-buyer who has to face the consequences. Investigations are still going on to find out whether this is a hereditary problem or not. So far, the idea of a soaking wet and rather muddy dog does not appeal to you, you have to teach him right from the start to stay away from the water. Do not think that will be easy! A walk without a swim is, in the eyes of a Cocker, only half a walk and if there's nowhere to swim, a deep muddy puddle may suit him just fine!

His energy is endless. He will walk the same distance as you two or three times over, at full speed, without resting, and it only takes the ten minutes' drive home from the park to restore him. Once home, he's ready for you to play with him, throw a ball for him to fetch or whatever it takes to get rid of his energy.

PHYSICAL CHARACTERISTICS

The Cocker is a relatively small, compact dog, with a height of between 15 and 16 inches and a weight of around 30 pounds. His small body, however, is big on strength and power—-two characteristics that are very important for a dog whose main function is to work in the field. For the pet, rather than the working, Cocker, this strength is evident in his boundless energy. This is a breed that never seems to tire, so be prepared to spend time participating in some type of physical activity with your Cocker. Not only will he appreciate the outlet for his energy, he will appreciate the time spent with you!

One of the most obvious and most striking physical characteristics of the breed is the coat. The coat is long, flat and silky, consisting of a top coat and an undercoat. The Cocker's dense coat does require attention in grooming, both to keep it looking in top condition and to prevent any odour. Perhaps the most interesting feature of the Cocker's coat is the wide variation of colours and colour patterns that are seen. Even more interesting is that there can

Although the Cocker is the smallest member of the Gundog Group, he was designed to work in the field and must do so tirelessly.

be personality differences within the breed based on coat colour! More detail about this aspect of the Cocker Spaniel is worth mentioning.

COAT COLOUR AND VARIATIONS

Dr. Caius mentioned in his *Treatis of Dogges* (1570) the Aquaticus or Spanyell, who finds game in the water and who is either red-and-white, solid black or solid red. Later, in 1803, in the book *The Sportsman's Cabinet,* springing spaniels and cocking spaniels are mentioned in the colours black-and-white, liver-and-white, red-and-white and a recent colour, seen on a dog imported from France, marble blue. Nowadays Cocker Spaniels occur in 17 different colours to be divided into two groups: the solids and the parti-colours.

There is sable-and-white in American Cockers, but so far I haven't seen this colour on an English Cocker Spaniel. The standard is not very explicit on colours, it just says 'various' and that in solids only a white patch is allowed on the chest.

Before the war it was common practice to breed all the colours together, but after the war the breeding was mainly solid to solid and parti-colour to parti-colour. In solids black is the dominant colour, with red and black-and-tan being recessive. In other words, if a dominant black (black not carry-ing the gene for red) is mated to a dominant black, all the puppies will be black. If the dominant black is mated to a black carrying the gene for red, all the puppies will also be black, but some of them will be carrying the gene for red. If two blacks, both carrying the gene for red are mated, theoretically 25% of the puppies will be dominant black, 50% will be black but carrying the gene for red and 25% will be red (fig. 1). If a red is mated to a black with the gene for red, 50% will be red and 50% will be black (fig. 2). Two reds mated together can only produce red.

To produce liver, both parents should—apart from the gene for liver—also have the gene for black. If two dogs with the gene for liver but without the gene for black were to be mated, the resulting puppies would all be red with brown pigmentation (instead of black). A liver dog with the gene for liver and for black mated to a black or a red without the gene for liver will only produce black puppies (fig. 3). Liver pups can only be the result of a liver to liver or liver to brown-pigmented-red combination (fig. 4). A liver dog with the gene for red mated to a red or black with the gene for red will produce red puppies (fig. 5). A liver mated to a black-pigmented red (without the gene for liver) gives 25 to 50% black pups. This is the only way to breed black

Expected Colours in Purebred Cocker Spaniels

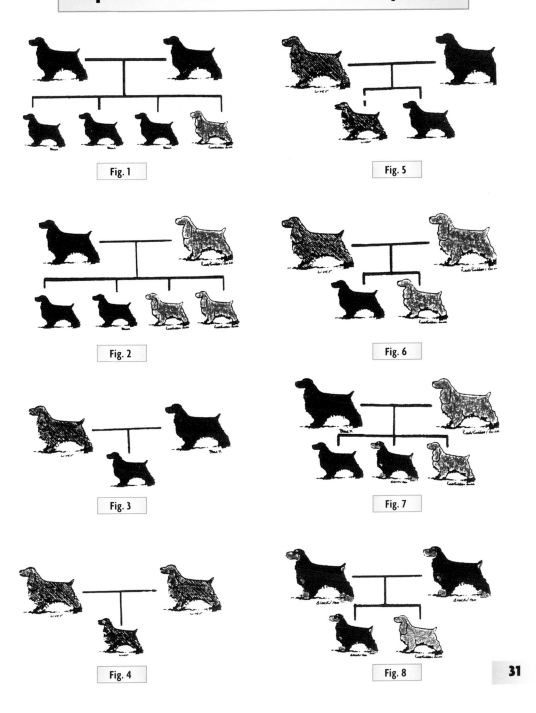

Fig. 1

Fig. 2

Fig. 3

Fig. 4

Fig. 5

Fig. 6

Fig. 7

Fig. 8

Expected Colours in Purebred Cocker Spaniels

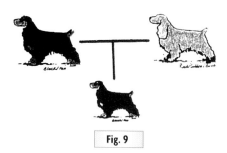

Fig. 9

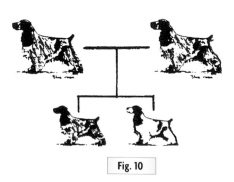

Fig. 10

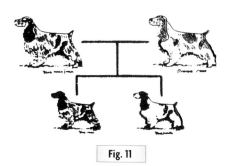

Fig. 11

puppies out of non-black parents (fig. 6).

Black-and-tans and liver-and-tans are in fact solids with recessive genes for tan. Solid is dominant and the tan pattern is recessive. The tan markings are genetically fixed, but the quantity of tan can differ greatly as can the shade of tan. The only way to see whether a dog possesses the gene for tan is by breeding. A black-and-red may both have the gene for tan and produce blacks, reds and black-and-tans (fig. 7). Two black-and-tans produce 75% black-and-tan puppies. Should both of them have the gene for red, then 25% of the pups would be red-and-tan, but in practice this is invisible (fig. 8). However, if such dogs were to be mated to black-and-tans without the gene for red, the offspring would be 100% black-and-tan (fig. 9).

In parti-colours, blue roan is dominant over all other parti-colours. Roan is dominant over ticking, but ticking is dominant over black-and-white or orange-and-white. Dark blue roan is dominant over light blue roan, which explains why we see so many more dark blue roans than black-and-whites or light blues. I bred three litters with a black-and-white bitch out of a black-and-white mother. All three sires were blue (with black-and-whites in their pedigrees) and of all three litters I had only one black-and-white. To have black-and-white puppies out of her, I would have had to mate her to a black-and-white or orange-and-white dog (fig. 10).

A black-and-white is, in fact, a black dog with two genes for parti-colour. Should he have one gene for roan and one for open-marked white, he himself would be a roan. A black-and-tan with two genes for parti-colour becomes a tri-colour or blue-roan-and-tan. If we breed an orange roan bitch to a black-and-white dog, their puppies will nearly all be dark blue roan.

In a newborn litter of parti-colours all of the puppies are black-and-white (or orange-and-white). The only way to see whether the puppy will later become a blue roan is by looking at his pads and nails. Should these be black right from the start, then you know that your puppy will be a blue roan. If they are pink, then the puppy will become a black-and-white. To produce tri-colour puppies, both parents should have the gene for tan. The tan is only there where the markings are. Should you have a puppy with an irregular marking (i.e., one black eye/ear and one white eye/ear) the tan will only be found on the side where the black marking is. This is not a fault according to the standard, but most breeders do not like it.

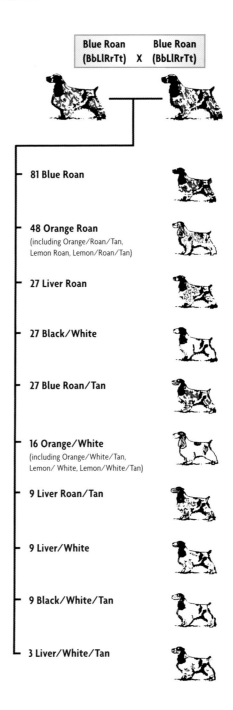

Blue Roan (BbLlRrTt) X Blue Roan (BbLlRrTt)

81 Blue Roan

48 Orange Roan
(including Orange/Roan/Tan, Lemon Roan, Lemon/Roan/Tan)

27 Liver Roan

27 Black/White

27 Blue Roan/Tan

16 Orange/White
(including Orange/White/Tan, Lemon/White, Lemon/White/Tan)

9 Liver Roan/Tan

9 Liver/White

9 Black/White/Tan

3 Liver/White/Tan

The inheritance of colour in the Cocker Spaniel may seem somewhat complicated, but is well documented and understood by breeders.

We once mated a blue-roan-and-tan to an orange roan and the resulting puppies were all blue roan or black-and-white.

Conclusion? The blue-roan-and-tan missed the gene for orange and the orange roan missed the gene for tan (fig. 11). Although the puppies were blue, they all carried the gene for tan and for orange. Should we mate such a blue with these two genes to a liver roan, what will happen then? Chances are the whole litter is blue roan, but it might just be possible that you will have a 'rainbow' litter with every colour that's possible!

In parti-colours, the blue roan is dominant. These are blue roan siblings.

FACING PAGE: The *phenotype* of a Cocker is the colour that you see; the *genotype* is the colour carried by the genes, which may not be always apparent.

The Cocker Spaniel

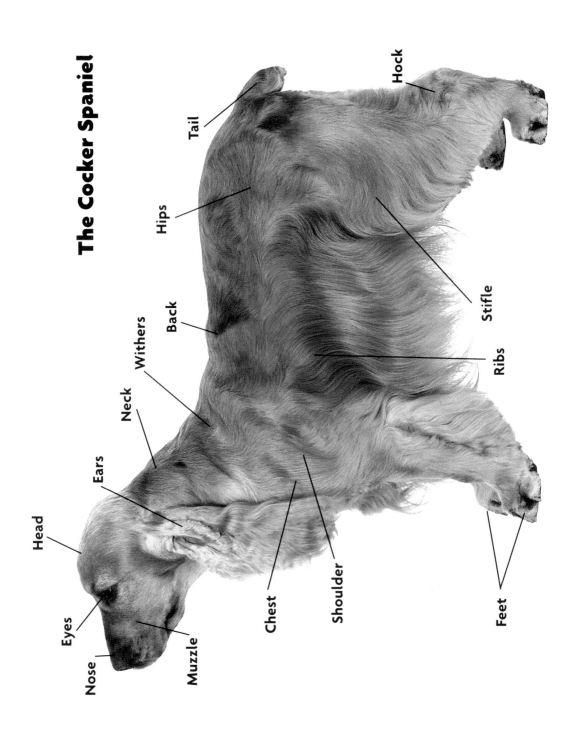

Head

Eyes

Nose

Muzzle

Ears

Neck

Withers

Back

Hips

Tail

Hock

Stifle

Ribs

Chest

Shoulder

Feet

Breed Standard for the Cocker Spaniel

The first breed standard was written and officially approved by The Kennel Club in Great Britain in 1902. In later years some minor changes were made but, on the whole, the standard has remained practically unaltered. The latest standard, given here, dates from 2007. This standard is also officially recognised in all FCI countries. The FCI (Fédération Cynologique Internationale) includes the kennel clubs in the following countries: nearly all Continental European countries, Argentina, Brazil, Chile, Colombia, Ecuador, Mexico, Panama, Paraguay, Peru, Puerto Rico, Dominican Republic, Uruguay and Venezuela and, furthermore, Israel, Morocco, South Korea, Japan, Philippines and Thailand. There are several other countries that are not affiliated with the FCI but are associated with it, such as Bulgaria, Cyprus, Greece, Rumania, San Marino, Bermuda, Bolivia, Costa Rica, Cuba, Guatemala, Honduras, Ireland, Hong Kong, India, Indonesia, Malaysia, Singapore, Sri Lanka, Taiwan, Madagascar, South Africa, Zimbabwe, Australia and New Zealand. In these countries the

How proud to wear the ribbons of a winner! This is a lovely Cocker.

(Inset) A closer look at a wonderful Cocker head.

37

British Standard is the official breed standard. The breed standard as approved by the American Kennel Club is slightly different, certainly more extensive and with a slight difference in the ideal size and weight.

THE KENNEL CLUB STANDARD FOR THE SPANIEL (COCKER)

General Appearance: Merry, sturdy, sporting; well balanced; compact; measuring approximately same from withers to ground as from withers to root of tail.

Characteristics: Merry nature with ever-wagging tail shows a typical bustling movement, particularly when following scent, fearless of heavy cover.

Temperament: Gentle and affectionate, yet full of life and exuberance.

Head and Skull: Square muzzle, with distinct stop set midway between tip of nose and occiput. Skull well developed, cleanly chiselled, neither too fine nor too coarse. Cheek bones not prominent. Nose sufficiently wide for acute scenting power.

This Cocker exhibits many positive qualities according to the standard. The dog illustrated in the inset possesses a moderate length of neck and long silky hair on the ears, as described in the standard.

Eyes: Full, but not prominent. Dark brown or brown, never light, but in the case of liver, liver roan and liver and white, dark hazel to harmonise with coat; with expression of intelligence and gentleness but wide awake, bright and merry; rims tight.

Ears: Lobular, set low on a level with eyes. Fine leathers extending to nose tip. Well clothed with long, straight silky hair.

Mouth: Jaws strong with a perfect, regular and complete scissors bite, i.e. upper teeth closely overlapping lower teeth and set square to the jaws.

Neck: Moderate in length, muscular. Set neatly into fine sloping shoulders. Clean throat.

Forequarters: Shoulders sloping and fine. Legs well boned, straight, sufficiently short for concentrated power. Not too short to interfere with tremendous exertions expected from this grand, sporting dog.

Body: Strong, compact. Chest well developed

38

Mother and daughter. The genetics of colour in the Cocker is an exciting aspect of breeding. Given the many possibilities, breeders enjoy the surprises that a litter can offer.

and brisket deep; neither too wide nor too narrow in front. Ribs well sprung. Loin short, wide with firm, level topline gently sloping downwards to tail from end of loin to set on of tail.

Hindquarters: Wide, well rounded, very muscular. Legs well boned, good bend of stifle, short below hock allowing for plenty of drive.

Feet: Firm, thickly padded, cat-like.

Tail: Set on slightly lower than line of back. Must be merry in action and carried level, never cocked up. Previously customarily docked. Docked: Never too short to hide, nor too long to interfere with, the incessant merry action when working. Undocked: Slightly curved, of moderate length, proportionate to size of body giving an overall balanced appearance; ideally not reaching below the hock. Strong at the root and tapering to a fine tip; well feathered in keeping with the coat. Lively in action, carried on a plane not higher than level of back and never so low as to indicate timidity.

Gait/Movement: True through action with great drive covering ground well.

Coat: Flat, silky in texture, never wiry or wavy, not too profuse and never curly. Well feathered forelegs, body and hindlegs above hocks.

Colour: Various. In self colours no white allowed except on chest.

Size: Height approximately: dogs 39–41 cms (15.5–16 ins), bitches 38–39 cms (15–15.5 ins). Weight approximately: 13–14.5 kgs (28–32 lbs).

Faults: Any departure from the foregoing points should be considered a fault and the seriousness with which the fault should be regarded should be in exact proportion to its degree and its effect upon the health and welfare of the dog.

Note: Male animals should have two apparently normal testicles fully descended into the scrotum.

The word 'various' in the standard refers not just to colour. The Cocker is seen in many interesting marking patterns as well.

EARS

Set on level with eyes; hair is long, straight and silky (left). Ears on right are too short.

HEAD

Should have moderately pronounced occiput (left). Skull on right is too round.

SKULL

Two examples of incorrect head: Skull longer than muzzle (left) and skull shorter than muzzle (right).

FEET

Should have straight, firm pasterns and round, thickly padded feet (left). On right, pastern is overly angulated and foot is elongated.

TAIL

Should be carried level (left), never cocked up (right).

Cockers get on well with children, though appropriate supervision is advised when children are handling their canine companions.

Let your children assist in the selection of your Cocker puppy. You, of course, must ensure that the puppy is healthy and sound and that the breed is suitable to your family's lifestyle.

Your Cocker Spaniel Puppy

CHOOSING YOUR PUPPY
You've decided that you want to share your life with a Cocker Spaniel. This is the breed that suits you best in temperament and in lifestyle. What do you plan to do with your new puppy? Do you want to work on your condition and that of your dog by joining agility classes? Would you like to do obedience training or are you so fortunate as to be able to take a dog on a shoot? Your choice of a Cocker Spaniel means that you will be able to do all of these things. By choosing a Cocker

DID YOU KNOW?
An important consideration to be discussed is the sex of your puppy. For a family companion, a Cocker Spaniel bitch is the better choice, considering the female's inbred concern for all young creatures and her accompanying tolerance and patience. If you do not intend to spay your pet when she has matured or is well over her growing period, then extra care is required during the times of her heat.

Spaniel, you have chosen a companion with a very happy temperament, who thinks life is wonderful and who will love you indiscriminately.

Now, before you go to a breeder there are a few questions that need to be answered. What colour do you like? There are a few considerations. A red one will usually have an easy coat that does not

Selecting the puppy best suited for your lifestyle is not easy. Keep in mind that you'll have the dog as a pet for about 10 to 14 years.

DID YOU KNOW?
Taking your dog from the breeder to your home in a car can be a very uncomfortable experience for both of you. The puppy will have been taken from his warm, friendly, safe environment and brought into a strange new environment. An environment that moves. Be prepared for loose bowels, urination, crying, whining and even fear biting. With proper love and encouragement when you arrive home, the stress of the trip should quickly disappear.

for the parti-colours: oranges usually do not have much surplus hair and only need occasional trimming of the head, ears, feet and tail, but blue roans have a heavier coat and will have to be trimmed every 6 to 8 weeks.

Colour is just one consideration. Will your Cocker Spaniel be a dog or a bitch? It is often said that a bitch is sweeter than a dog, but in my experience the dogs are just as sweet as the bitches and are also very easygoing.

Will it be a much-loved pet or would you like to show and maybe breed a litter in future? It is very important that you explain all of your preferences to the breeder so that he can help you pick the puppy that is best suited to you.

require too much trimming. Some blacks have natural non-trim coats, but the majority grows a lot of hair and have to be trimmed every 6 to 8 weeks. The same goes

Friendly Cocker puppies will rush to greet you. Never select the puppy that is shy or withdrawn. You want a Cocker that welcomes attention and human handling.

Compare the puppies to the dam. The comparison might give you some idea of the eventual colour, size and temperament of the puppy.

There is a very general difference in temperaments. The solids are highly intelligent and therefore need a firm hand. If you have a family with kids, it might be wiser not to buy a red or black puppy because in that case the puppy will have several 'masters' and will end up not listening to anybody! He may become a slightly dominant dog that may cause problems. The personalities of the puppies in a litter may differ slightly. Explain to the breeder what you prefer: the softer, sweeter one or the outgoing, cheeky puppy?

If you have the time and dedication to train your puppy and treat him consistently at all times, there is no better pet than a Cocker Spaniel.

Purchase the best puppy that you can afford. The 'bargain' puppy may cost you tenfold in veterinary expenses, behavioural consultations and heartbreak.

FINDING A BREEDER

Before getting into contact with a breeder, it may help you to visit a couple of dog shows or the breed club championship show. Watch the breeders and how they communicate with their dogs, look at the dogs and see which breeder has dogs with the type and tem-

47

DID YOU KNOW?

The majority of problems that are commonly seen in young pups will disappear as your Cocker Spaniel gets older. However, how you deal with problems when he is young will determine how he reacts to discipline as an adult dog. It is important to establish who is boss (hopefully it will be you!) right away when you are first bonding with your Cocker Spaniel. This bond will set the tone for the rest of your life together.

perament you like. You can also contact the breed club and ask for names and addresses of breeders with puppies for sale. The club will give you a list of breeders who have puppies that fulfil the club rules. These rules mainly concern matters of hereditary defects in both parents. If the breeders whose dogs you like are not on the list, do not hesitate to contact them and ask if they will have puppies in the future and whether these puppies will fulfil the club rules. If you visit a breeder and you are a bit doubtful about the puppies, the breeder or the conditions in which the puppies are kept, or if the breeder thinks that checking for hereditary defects is not necessary, do not buy! It must be a 100-percent decision—-buying because you are afraid to say no or because you feel sorry for the pup is wrong. After all, you are going to

A good way to get a Cocker puppy is to visit a dog show and find the dog that strikes your fancy. Contact the breeder to find out about obtaining a pup from the same bloodline.

You can buy your dog when it is very young, but responsible breeders will not separate a pup from its dam until it is at least eight weeks old.

buy a companion for the next 12 to 14 years and you must be absolutely sure that he is the one you want and no other!

Should you want to buy a puppy for showing, discuss this with the breeder. Also discuss with him what to do in case the puppy will not be showable. Unforeseen changes may happen as the pup grows, and if you are very determined to have a show quality pup you might do better to buy a more mature puppy, say 6 to 7 months old, so that these risks cannot occur.

Whether you are buying a pup for pet or for show, it is equally important to find out about the pup's medical back-

DID YOU KNOW?
Your puppy should have a well-fed appearance but not a distended abdomen, which may indicate worms or incorrect feeding, or both. The body should be firm, with a solid feel. The skin of the abdomen should be pale pink and clean, without signs of scratching or rash. Check the hind legs to make certain that dewclaws were removed, if any were present at birth.

ground. Inquire about inoculations and when the puppy was last dosed for worms.

49

Raising a litter of Cockers is time-consuming, food-consuming and money-consuming. Good breeders rarely make any profit on puppy sales. For true breeders, a litter is a labour of love and the pursuit of excellence.

It is nowadays common practice to sell a puppy with a sales contract. This is fine, but do not sign on the spot. Ask the breeder if you can take it home to read it carefully so that you know exactly what you are going to sign. More important than a sales contract, however, is a good relationship between you and the breeder. A responsible, dedicated breeder is at all times willing to answer all your questions, to calm your fears and to share your joys.

BUYING YOUR PUPPY

You have contacted a breeder, he has a litter and there you are, surrounded by all these lovely puppies. How will you ever be able to choose? For instance, if you have decided you want a bitch puppy, ask the breeder to take the dog puppies away to make the choice a bit easier. Now what you are looking for is a healthy, good-looking, happy little thing that will be all over you in no time when you crouch down, thinking you are great fun. Do not go for a shy pup, but do not go for a bully either. Ask the breeder if you can see the dam (and sire if possible) and see what her temperament is like. Discuss the pedigree with him so that you can make sure that your puppy comes from good stock.

DID YOU KNOW?

Two important documents you will get from the breeder are the pup's pedigree and registration papers. The breeder should register the litter and each pup with The Kennel Club, and it is necessary for you to have the paperwork to transfer ownership to yourself. If you are purchasing a pup that is not eligible for the Breed Register, you can still register your pup on the Activity Register, which will enable you to compete in competitions licensed by The Kennel Club, i.e. Obedience, Working Trials, Agility, Heelwork to Music and Flyball. You will not be able to show your dog or be eligible to compete in Field Trials or Gundog Working Tests.

It may seem like a lot of effort…and you have not even brought the pup home yet! Remember, though, you cannot be too careful when it comes to deciding on the type of dog you want and finding out about your prospective pup's background. Buying a puppy is not—or should not be—just another whimsical purchase. In fact, this is one instance in which you actually do get to choose your own family! But, you may be thinking, buying a puppy should be fun—it should not be so serious and so much work. If you keep in mind the thought that your puppy is not a cuddly stuffed toy or decorative lawn ornament, but instead will become a real member of your family, you will realise that while buying a puppy is a pleasurable and exciting endeavour, it is not something to be taken lightly. Relax…the fun will start when the pup comes home!

Always keep in mind that a puppy is nothing more than a

DID YOU KNOW?
Unfortunately, when a puppy is purchased by someone who does not take into consideration the time and attention that dog ownership requires, it is the puppy who suffers when he is either abandoned or placed in a shelter by a frustrated owner. So all of the 'homework' you do in preparation for your pup's arrival will benefit you both. The more informed you are, the more you will know what to expect and the better equipped you will be to handle the ups and downs of raising a puppy. Hopefully, everyone in the household is willing to do his part in raising and caring for the pup. The anticipation of owning a dog often brings a lot of promises from excited family members: 'I will walk him every day,' 'I will feed him,' 'I will housebreak him,' etc., but these things take time and effort, and promises can easily be forgotten once the novelty of the new pet has worn off.

The larger the puppies grow, they more they cost the breeder, so be considerate. Buying a Cocker puppy is a VERY serious commitment. Don't be hasty or take it lightly.

This Cocker puppy is only a few days old. The eyes are closed for the first week and the ears lie backwards, flat against the head.

baby in a furry disguise...a baby who is virtually helpless in a human world and who trusts his owner for fulfilment of his basic needs for survival. That goes beyond food, water and shelter; your pup needs care, protection, guidance and love. If you are not prepared to commit to this, then you are not prepared to own a dog.

Do not worry too much about it though; you will probably find that once your pup gets used to his new home, he will fall into his place in the family quite naturally. But it never hurts to emphasise the commitment of dog ownership. With some time

and patience, it is really not too difficult to raise a curious and exuberant Cocker Spaniel pup to be a well-adjusted and well-mannered adult dog—a dog that could be your most loyal friend.

PREPARING PUPPY'S PLACE IN YOUR HOME

Researching your breed and finding a breeder are only two aspects of the 'homework' you will have to do before bringing your puppy home. You will also have to prepare your home and family for the new addition. Much like you would prepare a nursery for a newborn baby, you will need to designate a place in your home that will be the puppy's own. How you prepare your home will depend on how much freedom the dog will be allowed: will he be confined to one room or a specific area in the house, or will he be allowed to roam as he pleases? Will he spend most of his time in the house or will he be primarily an

Does anything feel better than holding your new puppy? The puppy is probably just as happy as you are.

outdoor dog? Whatever you decide, you must ensure that he has a place that he can 'call his own.'

When you bring your new puppy into your home, you are bringing him into what will become his home as well. Obviously, you did not buy a puppy so that he could take over your house, but in order for a puppy to grow into a stable, well-adjusted dog, he has to feel comfortable in his surroundings. Remember, he is leaving the warmth and security of his mother and littermates, plus the familiarity of the only place he has ever known, so it is important to make his transition as easy as possible. By preparing a place in your home for the puppy, you are making him feel as welcome as possible in a strange new place. It should not take him long to get used to it, but the sudden shock of being transplanted is somewhat traumatic for a young pup. Imagine how a small child would feel in the same situation—that is how your puppy must be feeling. It is up to you to reassure him and to let him know, 'Little fellow, you are going to like it here!'

WHAT YOU SHOULD BUY
CRATE
To someone unfamiliar with the use of crates in dog training, it may seem like punishment to

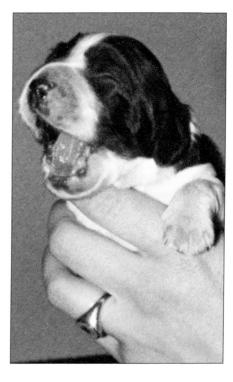

A week-old puppy whose eyes are just starting to open.

shut a dog in a crate; this is not the case at all. Crates are not cruel—crates have many humane and highly effective uses in dog care and training. For example, crate training is a very popular and very successful house-training method; a crate can keep your dog safe during travel; and, perhaps most importantly, a crate provides your dog with a place of his own in your home. It serves as a 'doggie bedroom' of sorts—your Cocker can curl up in his crate when he wants to sleep or when he just needs a break. Many dogs sleep in their crates overnight. When lined

Photo by Mikki Pet Products.

type. For example, a wire crate is more open, allowing the air to flow through and affording the dog a view of what is going on around him. A fibreglass crate, however, is sturdier and can double as a travel crate since it provides more protection for the dog. The size of the crate is another thing to consider. Puppies do not stay puppies forever—in fact, sometimes it seems as if they grow right before your eyes. Unless you have the money and the inclination to buy a new crate every time your pup has a growth spurt, it is better to get one that will accommodate your dog both as a pup and at full size.

BEDDING

A blanket or two, or more ideally a vetbed, in the dog's crate

with soft blankets and filled with his favourite toys and stuffed pals, a crate becomes a cosy pseudo-den for your dog. Like his ancestors, he too will seek out the comfort and retreat of a den—you just happen to be providing him with something a little more luxurious than leaves and twigs lining a dirty ditch.

As far as purchasing a crate, the type that you buy is up to you. It will most likely be one of the two most popular types: wire or fibreglass. There are advantages and disadvantages to each

will help the dog feel more at home. First, the blankets will take the place of the leaves, twigs, etc., that the pup would use in the wild to make a den; the pup can make his own 'burrow' in the crate. Although your pup is far removed from his den-making ancestors, the denning instinct is still a part of his genetic makeup. Second, until you bring your pup home, he has been sleeping amidst the warmth of his mother and litter-mates, and while a blanket is not the same as a warm, breathing body, it still provides heat and something with which to snuggle. You will want to wash your pup's blankets frequently in case he has an accident in his crate and replace or remove any blanket that becomes ragged and starts to fall apart.

DID YOU KNOW?

During crate training, you should partition off the section of the crate in which the pup stays. If he is given too big of an area, this will hinder your training efforts. Crate training is based on the fact that a dog does not like to soil his sleeping quarters, so it is ineffective to keep a pup in a crate that is so big that he can eliminate in one end and get far enough away from it to sleep. Also, you want to make the crate den-like for the pup. Blankets and a favourite toy will make the crate cosy for the small Cocker Spaniel; as he grows, you may want to evict some of his 'room-mates' to make more room.

It will take some coaxing at first, but be patient. Given some time to get used to it, your pup will adapt to his new home-within-a-home quite nicely.

Toys

Toys are a must for dogs of all ages, especially for curious playful pups. Puppies are the 'children' of the dog world, and what child does not love toys? Chew toys provide enjoyment to both dog and owner—your dog will enjoy playing with his favourite toys, while you will enjoy the fact that they distract him from your expensive shoes and leather sofa. Puppies love to chew; in fact, chewing is a physical need for

Puppies love to cuddle up. Be sure to get nice warm bedding for your puppy. If possible, bring some familiar bedding home from the breeder. The scent will make the puppy feel more at ease in his new surroundings.

pups as they are teething, and everything looks appetising! The full range of your possessions—from old dishrag to Oriental rug—are fair game in the eyes of a teething pup. Puppies are not all that discerning when it comes to finding something to literally 'sink their teeth into'—everything tastes great!

Stuffed toys are another option; these are good to put in the dog's crate to give him some company. Be careful of these, as a pup can de-stuff one

DID YOU KNOW?

With a big variety of dog toys available, and so many that look like they would be a lot of fun for a dog, be careful in your selection. It is amazing what a set of puppy teeth can do to an innocent-looking toy, so, obviously, safety is a major consideration. Be sure to choose the most durable products that you can find. Hard nylon bones and toys are a safe bet, and many of them are offered in different scents and flavours that will be sure to capture your dog's attention. It is always fun to play a game of catch with your dog, and there are balls and flying discs that are specially made to withstand dog teeth.

pretty quickly, and stay away from stuffed toys with small plastic eyes or parts that a pup could choke on. Similarly, squeaky toys are quite popular. There are dogs that will come running from anywhere in the house at the first sound from their favourite squeaky friend. Again, if a pup de-stuffs one of these, the small plastic squeaker inside can be dangerous if swallowed. Monitor the condition of your pup's toys carefully and get rid of any that have been chewed to the point of becoming potentially dangerous.

Be careful of natural bones, which have a tendency to splinter into sharp, dangerous pieces. Also be careful of rawhide, which after enough chewing can turn into pieces that are easy to swallow, and also watch out for the mushy mess it can turn into on your carpet. Most puppies love the calf hooves that you can

By nature, Cockers are soft-mouthed dogs and generally appreciate soft, plush toys for play. Often a puppy will select one special soft toy as his favourite.

buy in any pet shop or at shows. They can chew for hours on them without coming to any harm. However, if what's left of the hoof becomes too small you'd better take it away.

LEAD
A nylon lead is probably the best option as it is the most resistant to puppy teeth should your pup take a liking to chewing on his lead. Of course, this is a habit that should be nipped in the bud, but if your pup likes to chew on his lead he has a very slim chance of being able to chew through the strong nylon. Nylon leads are also lightweight,

Your local pet shop will have a large variety of leads in different colours and made from different materials.

which is good for a young
Cocker puppy who is just getting
used to the idea of walking on a
lead. For everyday walking and
safety purposes, the nylon lead
is a good choice. As your pup
grows up and gets used to walking on the lead, and can do it
politely, you may want to purchase a flexible lead, which
allows you either to extend the
length to give the dog a broader
area to explore or to pull in the
lead when you want to keep him
close.

COLLAR

Your pup should get used to wear-
ing a collar because the lead and
collar go hand in hand—you have
to attach the lead to something! A
lightweight nylon collar will be a
good choice; make sure that it fits
snugly enough so that the pup

A lightweight
nylon collar is
the best choice
for your Cocker
puppy.

cannot wriggle out of it, but loose
enough so that it will not be
uncomfortably tight around the
pup's neck. You should be able to
fit a finger in between the pup and
the collar. It may take some time
for your pup to get used to wear-
ing the collar, but soon he will not
even notice that it is there.

FOOD AND WATER BOWLS

Your pup will need two bowls,
one for food and one for water.
You may want two sets of bowls,
one for inside and one for outside,
depending on where the dog will
be fed and where he will be
spending most of his time.
Stainless steel bowls are good, but

An orange roan Cocker puppy. The colour will slowly become darker and more intense.

Your local pet shop will be able to offer you a large variety of food and water bowls.

the sturdy special Spaniel bowls whose shape allows the ears to fall outside the bowl are popular choices. These bowls save you from messy ears after dinner and a wet floor after drinking! Plastic bowls are very chewable and therefore not advisable. Some dog owners like to put their dogs' food and water bowls on a specially made elevated stand; this brings the food closer to the dog's level so he does not have to bend down as far, thus aiding his digestion and helping to guard against bloat or gastric torsion in deep-chested dogs. The most important thing is to buy sturdy bowls since, again, anything is in danger of being

Photo by Mikki Pet Products.

Thin collars and leads are often used for showing a dog, but you will need something more durable for everyday walks.

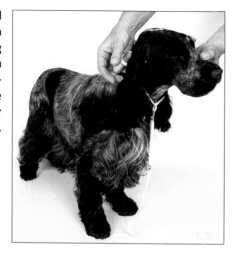

chewed by puppy teeth and you do not want your dog to be constantly chewing apart his bowl (for his safety and for your wallet!).

CLEANING SUPPLIES

A pup that is not housetrained means you will be doing a lot of cleaning until he is. Accidents will occur, which is okay for now because he does not know any better. All you can do is clean up any 'accidents'—old rags, towels, newspapers and a safe disinfectant are good to have on hand.

BEYOND THE BASICS

The items previously discussed are the bare necessities. You will find out what else you need as you go along—grooming supplies, flea/tick protection, baby gates to partition a

Pet shops sell special food and water bowls designed to keep the dog's ears out of the bowl when it is eating or drinking. These bowls are ideal for dogs like Cockers that have hanging, furry ears.

60

room, etc.—these things will vary depending on your situation. It is just important that right away you have everything you need to feed and make your Cocker Spaniel comfortable in his first few days at home.

PUPPY-PROOFING YOUR HOME

Aside from making sure that your puppy will be comfortable in your home, you also have to make sure that your home is safe for your pup. This means taking precautions to make sure that your pup will not get into anything he should not get into and that there is nothing within his reach that may harm him should he sniff it, chew it, inspect it, etc. This probably seems obvious since, while you are primarily concerned with your pup's safety, at the same time you do not want your belongings to be ruined. Breakables should be placed out of reach if your dog is to have full run of the house. If he is to be limited to certain places

Cocker puppies are very curious. They pick up and taste everything. Be certain that there are no dangerous plants in your garden that your puppy could eat.

within the house, keep any potentially dangerous items in the 'off-limits' areas. An electrical wire can pose a danger should the puppy decide to taste it—and who is going to convince a pup that it would not make a great chew toy? Cables should be fastened tightly against the wall. If your dog is going to spend time in a crate, make sure that there is nothing near his crate that he can reach if he sticks his curious little nose or paws through the openings. And just as you would with a child, keep all household cleaners and chemicals where the pup cannot get to them.

It is just as important to make sure that the outside of your home is safe. Of course your puppy should never be unsupervised, but a pup let loose in the garden will want to run and explore, and he should be granted that freedom. Do not let a fence give you a false sense of security; you would be surprised how crafty (and persistent) a dog can be in figuring out how to dig under and squeeze his way through small holes, or to jump or climb over a fence. The remedy is to make the fence high

A very alert blue roan and tan Cocker Spaniel puppy. Don't let the angelic look fool you. This industrious little puppy can make quite a mess without proper supervision.

61

enough so that it really is impossible for your dog to get over it (about 3 metres should suffice) and well embedded into the ground. Be sure to repair or secure any gaps in the fence. Check the fence periodically to ensure that it is in good shape and make repairs as needed; a very determined pup may return to the same spot to 'work on it' until he is able to get through.

You cannot teach an old dog new tricks is an untrue expression. However, it is a lot easier to train a puppy than to untrain an adult dog.

FIRST TRIP TO THE VET
Okay, you have picked out your puppy, your home and family are ready, now all you have to do is pick your Cocker up from the breeder and the fun begins, right? Well...not so fast. Something else you need to prepare for is your pup's first trip to the veterinary surgeon. Perhaps the breeder can recommend someone in the area or maybe some other dog-owners can suggest a good vet. Either way, you should have an appointment arranged for your pup before you

pick him up; plan on taking him for a checkup within the first few days of bringing him home.

The pup's first visit will consist of an overall examination to make sure that the pup does not have any problems that are not apparent to the eye. The veterinary surgeon will also set up a schedule for the pup's vaccinations; the breeder will inform you of which ones the pup has already received and the vet can continue from there.

INTRODUCTION TO THE FAMILY
Everyone in the house will be excited about the puppy coming home and will want to pet him and play with him, but it is best to make the introduction low-key so as not to overwhelm the puppy. He is apprehensive already; it is the first time he has been separated from his mother and the breeder, and the ride to your home is likely the first time he has been in a car. The last thing you want to do is smother him, as this will only frighten him further. This is not to say that human contact is not extremely necessary at this stage, because this is the time when an instant connection between the pup and his human family are formed. Gentle petting and soothing words should help console him, as well as just putting him down and letting him explore on

his own (under your watchful eye, of course).

The pup may approach the family members or may busy himself with exploring for awhile. Gradually, each person should spend some time with the pup, one at a time, crouching down to get as close to the pup's level as possible and letting him sniff their hands and petting him gently. He definitely needs human attention and he needs to be touched—this is how to form an immediate bond. Just remember that the pup is experiencing a lot of things for the first time, all at the same time. There are new people, new noises, new smells, and new things to investigate, so be gentle, be affectionate and be as comforting as you can be.

This pensive black Cocker puppy has just been brought into his new home. How frightening it must be for him. Keep activities low key until the puppy becomes acquainted with his new family.

YOUR PUP'S FIRST NIGHT HOME

You have travelled home with your new charge safely in his basket or crate. He's been to the vet for a thorough check-over; he's been weighed, his papers examined; perhaps he's even been vaccinated and wormed as well. He's met the family, licked the whole family, including the excited children and the less-than-happy cat. He's explored his area, his new bed, the garden and anywhere else he's been permitted. He's eaten his first meal at home and relieved himself in the proper place. He's heard lots of new sounds, smelled new friends and seen more of the outside world than ever before.

That was the just the first day! He's worn out and is ready for bed...or so you think!

It's puppy's first night and you are ready to say 'Good night'—keep in mind that this is puppy's first night ever to be sleeping alone. His dam and littermates are no longer at paw's length away and he's a bit scared, cold and lonely. Be reassuring to your new family member. This is not the time to spoil him and give in to his inevitable whining.

Puppies whine. They whine to let the others know where they are and hopefully to get company out of it. Place your pup in his new bed or crate in his room and close the door. Mercifully, he will fall asleep without a peep. If the inevitable occurs, ignore the whining; he is fine. Be strong and keep his interest in mind. Do not allow

DID YOU KNOW?
You will probably start feeding your Cocker Spaniel pup the same food that he has been getting from the breeder; the breeder should give you a few days' supply to start you off. Although you should not give your pup too many treats, you will want to have puppy treats on hand for coaxing, training, rewards, etc. Be careful, though, as a small pup's calorie requirements are relatively low and a few treats can add up to almost a full day's worth of calories without the required nutrition.

your heart to become guilty and visit the pup. He will fall asleep.

Many breeders recommend placing a piece of bedding from his former homestead in his new bed so that he recognises the scent of his littermates. Others still advise placing a hot water bottle in his bed for warmth. This latter may be a good idea provided the pup doesn't attempt to suckle—he'll get good and wet and may not fall asleep so fast.

Puppy's first night can be somewhat stressful for the pup and his new family. Remember that you are setting the tone of nighttime at your house. Unless you want to play with your pup every evening at 10 p.m., midnight and 2 a.m., don't initiate the

Puppies need rest. Even the most feisty of Cocker puppies will need to take a nap after lots of activity.

habit. Surely your family will thank you, and so will your pup!

PREVENTING PUPPY PROBLEMS

SOCIALISATION

Now that you have done all of the preparatory work and have helped your pup get accustomed to his new home and family, it is about time for you to have some fun! Socialising your Cocker pup gives you the opportunity to show off your new friend, and your pup gets to reap the benefits of being an adorable furry creature that people will fuss over, want to pet and, in general, think is absolutely precious!

Besides getting to know his new family, your puppy should be exposed to other people, animals and situations. This will help him become well adjusted as he grows

The human touch is key to socialising a puppy.

Kissing, however, is not advised.

> **DID YOU KNOW?**
> The cost of food must also be mentioned. This is not a breed that can be maintained on table scraps and light supplement. Cocker Spaniels need a good supply of protein to develop the bone and muscle required in a working animal. Cocker Spaniels are not picky eaters but unless fed properly they can quickly succumb to skin problems.

up and less prone to being timid or fearful of the new things he will encounter. Your pup's socialisation began at the breeder's, now it is your responsibility to continue. The socialisation he receives up until the age of 12 weeks is the most critical, as this is the time when he forms his impressions of the outside world. Lack of socialisation can manifest itself in fear and aggression as the dog grows up. He needs lots of human interaction, affection, handling and exposure to other animals. Be careful during the eight-to-ten-week period, also known as the fear period. The interaction he receives during this time should be gentle and reassuring.

Once your pup has received

DID YOU KNOW?

Thorough socialisation includes not only meeting new people but also being introduced to new experiences such as riding in the car, having his coat brushed, hearing the television, walking in a crowd—the list is endless. The more your pup experiences, and the more positive the experiences are, the less of a shock and the less scary it will be for your pup to encounter new things.

When raised with kindness and love, your Cocker puppy will grow up to become a trusted member of your family.

during this very formative stage will impact his attitude toward future encounters. A pup that has a bad experience with a child may grow up to be a dog that is shy around or aggressive toward children, and you want your dog to be comfortable around everyone.

CONSISTENCY IN TRAINING

Dogs, being pack animals, naturally need a leader or else they try to establish dominance in

his necessary vaccinations, feel free to take him out and about (on his lead, of course). Take him around the neighbourhood, take him on your daily errands, let people pet him, let him meet other dogs and pets, etc. Puppies do not have to try to make friends; there will be no shortage of people who will want to introduce themselves. Just make sure that you carefully supervise each interaction. If the neighbourhood children want to say hello, for example, that is great—children and pups most often make great companions. But sometimes an excited child can unintentionally handle a pup too roughly, or an overzealous pup can playfully nip a little too hard. You want to make socialisation experiences positive ones; what a pup learns

A quality-bred Cocker puppy shines through. These two pups obviously have much talent and heart to share with the right new owners.

their packs. When you bring a dog into your family, who becomes the leader and who becomes the 'pack' is entirely up to you! Your pup's intuitive quest for dominance, coupled with the fact that it is nearly impossible to look at an adorable pup, with his soulful eyes and his long ears, and not cave in, give the pup almost an unfair advantage in getting the upper hand! And a pup will definitely test the waters to see what he can and cannot get away with.

Do not give in to those pleading eyes—stand your ground when it comes to disciplining the pup and make sure that all family members do the same. It will only confuse the pup when Mother tells him to get off the couch when he is used to sitting up there with Father to watch the nightly news. Avoid discrepancies by having all members of the household decide on the rules before the pup even comes home...and be consistent in enforcing them! Early training shapes the dog's personality, so you cannot be unclear in what you expect.

COMMON PUPPY PROBLEMS
The best way to prevent problems is to be proactive in stopping an undesirable behaviour as soon as it starts. The old saying 'You can't teach an old dog new tricks' does not necessarily hold true, but it is true that it is much easier to discourage bad behaviour in a young developing pup than to wait until the pup's bad behaviour becomes the adult

dog's bad habit. There are some problems that are especially prevalent in puppies as they develop.

NIPPING
As puppies start to teethe, they feel the need to sink their teeth into anything...unfortunately that includes your fingers, arms, hair, toes...whatever happens to be available. You may find this behaviour cute for about the first five seconds...until you feel just how sharp those puppy teeth

A seven-week-old black Cocker puppy in an alert stance. Something has caught his attention.

Well-bred puppies come to you after eight to ten weeks of constant care and affection. It is up to you to resume this attention and train them to become the best Cockers they can be. Are you up to a challenge like that?

are. This is something you want to discourage immediately and consistently with a firm 'No!' (or whatever number of firm 'No's' it takes for him to understand that you mean business) and replace your finger with an appropriate chew toy. While this behaviour is merely annoying when the dog is still young, it can become highly unpleasant as your Cocker Spaniel's adult teeth grow in and his jaws develop, if he thinks that it is okay to gnaw on human appendages.

CRYING/WHINING
Your pup will often cry, whine, whimper, howl or make some type of commotion when he is left alone. This is basically his way of calling out for attention, of calling

out to make sure that you know he is there and that you have not forgotten about him. He feels insecure when he is left alone, for example, when you are out of the house and he is in his crate or when you are in another part of the house and he cannot see you. The noise he is making is an expression of the anxiety he feels at being alone, so he needs to be taught that being alone is okay. You are not actually training the dog to stop making noise, you are training him to feel comfortable when he is alone and thus removing the need for him to make the noise. This is where the crate filled with cosy blankets and toys comes in handy. You want to know that he is safe when you are not there to supervise, and you know that he will be safe in his

69

A properly trained and cared-for Cocker Spaniel can bring you 14 years of devoted, loyal friendship.

DID YOU KNOW?

Chewing goes hand in hand with nipping in the sense that a teething puppy is always looking for a way to soothe his aching gums. In this case, instead of chewing on you, he may have taken a liking to your favourite shoe or something else which he should not be chewing. Again, realise that this is a normal canine behaviour that does not need to be discouraged, only redirected. Your pup just needs to be taught what is acceptable to chew on and what is off limits. Consistently tell him NO when you catch him chewing on something forbidden and give him a chew toy. Conversely, praise him when you catch him chewing on something appropriate. In this way you are discouraging the inappropriate behaviour and reinforcing the desired behaviour. The puppy chewing should stop after his adult teeth have come in, but most adult dogs continue to chew for various reasons—perhaps because he is bored, perhaps to relieve tension, or perhaps he just likes to chew. That is why it is important to redirect his chewing when he is still young.

crate rather than roaming freely about the house. In order for the pup to stay in his crate without making a fuss, he needs to be comfortable in his crate. On that note, it is extremely important that the crate is never used as a form of punishment, or the pup will have a negative association with the crate.

Accustom the pup to the crate in short, gradually increasing time intervals in which you put him in the crate, maybe with a treat, and stay in the room with him. If he cries or makes a fuss, do not go to him, but stay in his sight. Gradually he will realise that staying in his crate is all right without your help, and it will not be so traumatic for him when you are not around. You may want to leave the radio on softly when you leave the house; the sound of human voices may be comforting to him.

Everyday Care of Your Cocker Spaniel

FEEDING

You have probably heard it a thousand times, you are what you eat. Believe it or not, it's very true. For dogs, they are what you feed them because they have little choice in the matter. Even those people who truly want to feed their dogs the best often cannot do so because they do not know which foods are best for a dog.

There are four basic types of dog foods: fresh, preferably raw meat; dry food; semi-moist food and canned or tinned meat. For meat the most commonly used is tripe and dogs love it. You can combine their meat meals with dry food or with a semi-moist meal (dinner) or if fresh meat is not available, with tinned meat. Dry foods are less expensive but dogs often get bored with them. How would you

feel if you had the same meal day after day, year after year? Most dogs love vegetables and fruit and it certainly doesn't do them any harm to surprise them with a quarter of an apple, some leftover runner beans or lettuce.

PUPPY STAGE

When you decided to buy your puppy, the breeder probably told

You are what you eat! Be sure that whoever is responsible for feeding and watering the dog does a responsible job.

you what should feed the puppy once you bring him home. If he didn't, ask him. This is

DID YOU KNOW?

Many adult diets are based on grain. There is nothing wrong with this as long as it does not contain soy meal. Diets based on soy often cause flatulence (passing gas).

Grain-based diets are almost always the least expensive and a good grain diet is just as good as the most expensive diet containing animal protein.

There are many cases, however, when your dog might require a special diet. These special requirements should only be recommended by your veterinary surgeon.

important for two reasons; first, coming with you to live in totally new surroundings with so many new experiences is already a stressful experience for the puppy and a continuation of his diet will help him adjust. Even then his tummy may be upset the first couple of days, or he may even refuse to eat for a day or two, but don't worry about that. As soon as he is settled down he will eat again, especially if it's the food he has been used to. Second, the breeder most likely has a lot of experience in feeding mature dogs and puppies and keeping them in a peak condition, so it would be wise to listen to his advice. Most

breeders will provide you with an exact list of what to feed the puppy at which stage of his life and we strongly advise you to follow these instructions. Once your puppy is a mature 1- or 2-year-old, you can change his diet to what is more convenient for you (availability, costs, etc.), but with the growing puppy and youngster, stick to the breeder's diet. And remember that if ten breeders are discussing the feeding of their dogs, you will hear ten different opinions, and all of them will be right!

Your puppy will need 3 or 4 meals a day until he is about 9 months old, then you can cut back to two daily meals. Some people prefer to feed the adult dog once a day, but if your dog loves his food he probably won't go along with that. He might prefer to have a breakfast and a dinner.

ADULT DIETS
A dog is considered an adult when it has stopped growing. The growth is in height and/or length. Do not consider the dog's weight when the decision is made to switch from a puppy diet to a maintenance diet. Again you should rely on your breeder's advice. A Cocker Spaniel reaches adulthood at about two years of age, though some dogs are fully mature at 18 months while others may take up to three years.

Whatever you are going to feed your dog don't rely entirely on the quantities given in the manufacturer's instructions. Every dog has different requirements and—as in humans—where one dog will grow fat on just a small portion, another will need double the quantity. So it is best to 'feed with your eyes.'

DIETS FOR SENIOR DOGS

As dogs get older, their metabolism changes. The older dog usually exercises less, moves more slowly and sleeps more. This change in lifestyle and physiological performance requires a change in diet. Since these changes take place slowly, they might not be recognisable. What is easily recognisable is weight gain. By continually feeding your dog an adult maintenance diet when it is slowing down metabolically, your dog will gain weight. Obesity in an older dog compounds the health problems that already accompany old age. So here as well, feed 'with your eyes.'

As your dog gets older, few of his organs function up to par. The kidneys slow down and the intestines become less efficient. These age-related factors are best handled with a change in diet and a change in feeding schedule to give smaller portions that are more easily digested. There is no single best diet for every older dog; it is up to you to find out which diet suits his need best.

Young Cockers require a diet different from that of an adult dog. Since Cockers are considered a coat breed, a balanced diet is essential to maintaining a healthy coat.

DID YOU KNOW?

Selecting the best dry dog food is difficult. There is no majority consensus among veterinary scientists as to the value of nutrient analyses (protein, fat, fibre, moisture, ash, cholesterol, minerals, etc.). All agree that feeding trials are what matters, but you also have to consider the individual dog. Its weight, age, activity and what pleases its taste, all must be considered. It is probably best to take the advice of your veterinary surgeon. Every dog's dietary requirements vary, even during the lifetime of a particular dog.

If your dog is fed a good dry food, it does not require supplements of meat, vegetables, vitamins or minerals. The food should contain all that is necessary. Dogs do not get bored with the same diet. Give them the same food every day unless their status (age, activity, weight) changes.

Do you know what you are feeding your dog?

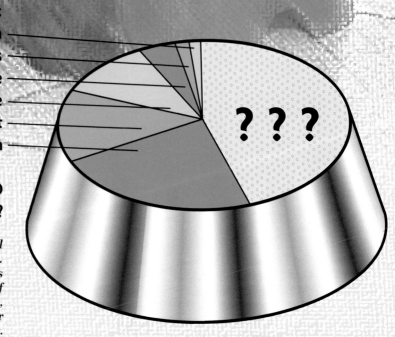

NUTRIENTS:
1.3% Calcium
1.6% Fatty Acids
4.6% Crude Fibre
11% Moisture
14% Crude Fat
22% Crude Protein

UNDOCUMENTED
45.5% ? ? ?

Read the label on your dog food. Most manufacturers merely advise you of 50-55% of the contents, leaving the other 45% in doubt.

? ? ?

DID YOU KNOW?

You must store your dry dog food carefully. Open packages of dog food quickly lose their vitamin value, usually within 90 days of being opened. Mould spores and vermin could also contaminate the food.

WATER

Just as your dog needs proper nutrition from his food, water is an essential "nutrient" as well. Water keeps the dog's body properly hydrated and promotes normal function of the body's systems. During house-training it is necessary to keep an eye on how much water your Cocker is drinking, but once he is reliably trained he should have access to clean fresh water at all times. Make sure that the dog's water bowl is clean, and change the water often.

You will find that your Cocker Spaniel is a very sloppy drinker! He loves his water bowl and in his enthusiasm he will often put not only his mouth but also both front paws in the bowl, or he will take one last mouthful of water and before swallowing it come to you to tell you how much he loves you! A special Spaniel bowl may help you keep the kitchen floor clean.

EXERCISE

All dogs require some form of exercise, regardless of breed. A sedentary lifestyle is as harmful to a dog as it is to a person. The Cocker Spaniel is a very lively and active breed that requires a lot of free exercise. He might like to come with you on a shopping expedition but what he needs is to run around free, preferably in

exciting surroundings like woods or fields, where he can develop his hunting instincts.

Owners often make mistakes in the exercise they give their dogs. Whereas the new puppy is an exciting thing, they tend to give him too much exercise. It is only human to show off with something you are very proud of, but it means that the small puppy is taken on too many walks. For a puppy up to 6 months, the garden is big enough. Take him to the park once a day to let him socialise and play with the other dogs for about 15 minutes. Once the puppy is about 9 months old you can extend the daily walks to

Spending a day in the field, hunting and retrieving birds, requires great stamina and strength. Although your Cocker may not get the chance to hunt, you should give him outlets for exercise and entertainment.

Retrieving is every Cocker's favourite pastime. The breed's coat is designed to withstand the water and provide insulation.

an hour daily, and once he is a year old his energy will be boundless.

We cannot stress the importance of exercise enough. It is essential to keep the dog's body fit, but it is also essential to

his mental well being. A bored dog will find something to do, which often manifests itself in some type of destructive behaviour. In this sense, it is essential for your mental well being as well!

GROOMING
BRUSHING
A natural bristle brush or a slicker brush can be used for regular routine brushing. Daily brushing is effective for removing dead hair and stimulating the dog's natural oils to add shine and a healthy look to the coat. Also, the soft and silky Spaniel coat can easily form tangles and mats, especially in places like the armpits and

The Cocker Spaniel's coat can easily tangle and become matted; a metal-toothed comb will keep the coat tidy.

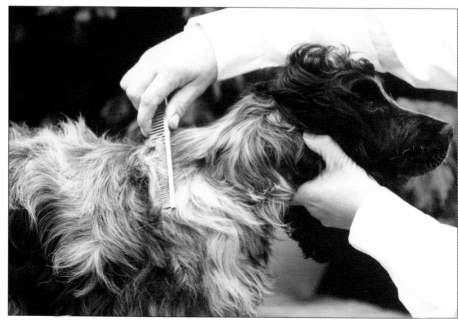

behind the ears and it is important to prevent these from forming.

TRIMMING AND PRESENTATION
When you buy your puppy he will have a smooth, short coat without much feathering, but by the time your puppy is five or six months old you'll find that he starts looking more like an Afghan Hound than a Cocker Spaniel! The coat grows fluffy, the feathering gets longer and he will have a big topknot and a long flag on his tail. With all of the hair on his feet he will bring a lot of mud and dirt into the house.

You must always remember that the coat of a Cocker Spaniel is to be hand-trimmed. Clipping and razoring is absolutely out of the question since it destroys the density of colour and you will never get that lovely, silky sheen that you get when you hand-trim the coat.

If you think you are not up to this job, you'll have to seek help. Ask the breeder whether he or she can help you; sometimes breeders use their (little) spare time to trim. If not, you'll have to take your puppy to a professional trimmer. Be very careful where you go, since beauty parlours often believe that their canine clients want nothing but to have all of their excess hair removed—and that means that the featherings on his legs go, his back is clipped

and the beautiful feathering on the ears is cut off. You have to stress the fact that what you want is a show trim— your Cocker

Introduce the Cocker puppy to grooming at an early age. Make your daily brushing sessions fun for the puppy.

Talk to your breeder or a professional groomer about the requirements of clipping your Cocker.

All grooming of Cocker Spaniels is done by hand and not with a clipper or a razor.

Selecting the best grooming tools is essential with Cockers. A slicker brush is ideal for removing dead hair and undercoat from your dog.

77

The hair on the feet and between the toes should be carefully trimmed with scissors.

A thin rubber glove or rubber fingertips assist in stripping the dead hairs from the dog's back. The gloves keep the hair from sliding through your fingers.

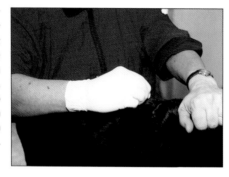

Serrated scissors or thinning shears, as they are sometimes called, are used to thin out dense tufts of hair that take away from your Cocker's outline.

must be shaped in the model in which he looks his best and this should be done by hand-plucking and not by scissoring or clippering.

The puppy's coat may take some time to get ready to come out; sometimes you have to wait until the puppy is 8 or 9 months old. This is annoying when you want to show the puppy, but be patient! Don't hurry the coat by using cutting instruments, you will regret that later.

What you should do in the meantime is groom your puppy regularly so that he is quite used to being on a table and being handled. Also, the abundant hair around the feet and between the pads on the underside can be cut away.

When you find that your puppy's coat may be ready to come out, you may find it easier to remove the hair by using 'thumblettes,' which fit over your thumb and forefinger, or thin surgical gloves, which are quite tight fitting.

Start with the head. Gently pull out the long hair, always pulling in the direction the hair grows. This sounds painful, but it is not, since what you pull out is dead hair. Start with just a couple of hairs so that your puppy can get used to the feel and so that you will not run the risk of hurting him by pulling out too many hairs at the same time. If you have a really smooth finish on top of the head, go to the top of the ears and remove the long hairs there, shaping around the back of the ear and about one-third of the way down. With your thinning scissors, cut carefully under the corner of the ear next to the head, and then thin out all long and surplus hair from the breastbone up to and including the throat.

Vets will often tell you that Cockers always have ear problems. This is not true. As long as you keep the inside of the ear clean and free of hair so that the ear can 'breathe' and, if necessary, use ear cleaner, you will find that you will have no problems with your Cocker's ears.

The neck must be trimmed out as short as possible, also with finger and thumb. If you use a fine-tooth comb regularly, you will find that it will remove nearly all of the puppy fluff. Try to use the comb as a stripper by gripping the hair between the comb and your thumb and pulling it toward you. It helps when you weave an elastic band between the teeth of the comb.

Continue down the shoulders until they are smooth and clear. The forelegs will have a lot of fluffy hair on the sides and the front. This must be removed. The feathering at the backside of the frontlegs stays as it is. The feathering should not touch the ground; when it does you can

shape it with the scissors. When viewed from the front, the feathering should lie backwards quite naturally from the elbow.

Work the comb with the elastic band through the body coat, the hair on the ribs and the outside of the hind legs. Pluck the fluffy hair that will not come out with the comb. Leave the feathering around the stifle. Trim the tail and cut underneath it. Pluck the hair down to where the feathering falls downwards and trim the feathering into shape. Shape the hair on the hock with the thinning scissors but do not take too much hair away; the hock should look full.

Grooming your Cocker for everyday maintenance compared to grooming a Cocker for a dog show requires different degrees of time and skill.

Trimming the feet is not easy and you have to be very careful. Start with lifting the foot and cutting out all the surplus hair from underneath. Cut closely around the outline of the foot. Then put the foot down and cut the surplus hair away that sticks

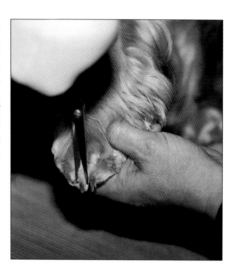

Trimming the feet is difficult. Always cut the hair in the direction of the toes. Consult a professional if you are unsure about trimming your dog.

up between the toes. Cut in the direction of the toes. Do not cut the hair in between the toes away, since that makes the foot look like a splayed foot. Finish off with a good brush and you will find that instead of a bundle of fluff you now have a Cocker with a beautiful, smooth and shining coat, gleaming with health and good condition.

BATHING

Dogs do not need to be bathed as often as humans, but sometimes a bath will be necessary. It is therefore important that you accustom your pup to being bathed as a puppy so that he is used to it when he grows up. You will have to bathe your dog the day before a show, and most owners like to bathe their bitches after they have been in season.

Before you are going to bathe your dog make sure that the coat is absolutely tangle-free. Make sure that your dog has a good non-slip surface to stand on. Begin by wetting the dog's coat. A shower or hose attachment is necessary for thoroughly wetting and rinsing the coat. Check the water temperature to make sure that it is neither too hot nor too cold. Fill his ear openings with cotton wool

DID YOU KNOW?

The use of human soap products like shampoo, bubble bath and soap can be very deleterious to a Cocker Spaniel's coat and skin. Human products are too strong and remove the protective oils coating the dog's hair and skin (making him water resistant).

Your Cocker Spaniel will need a bath when he gets a dirty coat or when the veterinary surgeon prescribes a medicated bath. In any case, only use shampoo made especially for dogs.

so that there is no chance of water or soap getting into the ear canals.

Next, apply shampoo to the dog's coat and work it into a good lather. You should purchase a shampoo that is made for dogs; do not use a product made for human hair. Wash the head last, as you do not want shampoo to drip into the dog's eyes while you are washing the rest of his body. Work the shampoo all the way down to the skin. You can use this opportunity to check the skin for any bumps, bites or other abnormalities. Do not neglect any area of the body—get all of the hard-to-reach places.

Once the dog has been thoroughly shampooed, he requires an equally thorough rinsing. Shampoo left in the coat can be irritating to the skin. Protect his eyes from the shampoo by shielding them with your hand and directing the flow of water in the opposite direction.

Be prepared for your dog to shake out his coat—you might want to stand back, but make sure you have a hold on the dog to keep him from running through the house.

Ear Cleaning

The ears should be kept clean and any excess hair inside the ear should be trimmed. Ears can be cleaned with an ear cleaner made especially for dogs. Be on the lookout for any signs of infections

Ears can be cleaned with an ear cleaner made specifically for dogs. Many Cockers suffer from minor ear infections (usually from mites) and should be checked by your vet.

or ear mite infestation and, during the summer, look for grass seeds that may be picked up by the ears and find their way into the ear canal. If your Cocker Spaniel has been shaking his head or scratching at his ears frequently, this usually indicates a problem. Don't clean the ear canal yourself. If you poke into the ear canal with

DID YOU KNOW?

Once you are sure that the dog is thoroughly rinsed, squeeze the excess water out of the coat with your hand and dry him with a heavy towel. You may choose to blow-dry his coat or just let it dry naturally. In cold weather, never allow your dog outside with a wet coat.

There are 'dry bath' products on the market, which are sprays and powders intended for spot cleaning, that can be used between regular baths, if necessary. They are not substitutes for regular baths, but they are easy to use for touch-ups as they do not require rinsing.

Routine ear cleaning should be done gently with a piece of soft cotton wool. Should you find parasites or blood, visit your vet immediately.

tweezers and cotton wool you'll only succeed in aggravating things. Contact your vet before the condition gets serious.

If you check your Spaniel's ears regularly and use the ear cleaner when the ear doesn't look 100% clean, you will find that the Spaniel's reputation for ear trouble is totally unfounded.

NAIL CLIPPING

Your Cocker should be accustomed to having his nails trimmed at an early age, since it will be part of your maintenance routine throughout his life. Not only does it look nicer but also a dog with long nails can cause injury if he jumps up or if he scratches someone unintentional-ly. Also, a long nail has a better chance of ripping and bleeding, or causing feet to spread. A good rule of thumb is that if you can hear your dog's nails clicking on the floor when he walks, his nails are too long.

Pet shops sell special clippers for dog's nails. These nail clippers assist you in not cutting into the 'quick,' the vein running through the nail.

Before you start cutting make sure you can identify the "quick" in each nail. The quick is a blood vessel that runs through the centre of each nail and grows rather close to the end. It will bleed profusely if accidentally cut, which will be quite painful for the dogs as it contains nerve endings. Keep some type of clotting agent on hand, such as a styptic pencil or styptic powder (the type used for shaving). This will stop the bleeding quickly when applied to the end of the cut nail. Do not panic if this happens, just stop the bleeding and talk soothingly to your dog. Once he has calmed down, move on to the next nail. It is better to clip a little at a time, particularly with black-nailed dogs.

Hold your pup steady as you begin trimming his nails; you do not want him to make any sudden movements or jump off the table. Talk to him soothingly and stroke his fur as you clip. Holding his foot in your hand, simply take off the end of each

puppies in his car for a visit to the vet or just for a ride, so that when you come to take your puppy home he knows what it is to be in a car. You will find that most Cockers love a ride in the car.

The best way for a dog to travel in a car is in his crate. You can use either the fibreglass or the wire crates. Another option is the specially made safety harness for dogs, which straps the dog in much like a seat belt. Do not let the dog roam loose in the vehicle—this is very dangerous! If you should stop short, your dog can be thrown and injured. If the dog starts climbing on you and pestering you while you are driving, you will not be able to

nail in one quick clip. You can purchase nail clippers that are specially made for dogs; you may find that the 'guillotine' type is the best type to use.

If you feel all this is beyond you, you might prefer the use of a nail grinder. This is a small, battery-operated contraption that slowly grinds the nails. There is no fear of cutting into the quick and the dogs don't mind the slight buzzing sound of the grinder at all.

TRAVELLING WITH YOUR DOG
You should accustom your Cocker Spaniel to riding in a car at an early age. If you are lucky, the breeder has already taken the

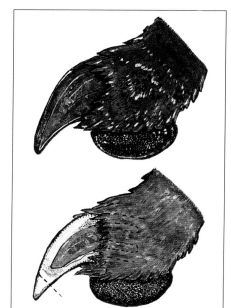

The dog's nail has a vein called the quick running through it. The quick is easier to see in light-coloured nails (bottom). To avoid cutting the quick, snip off the end of the nail a little at a time.

concentrate on the road. It is an unsafe situation for everyone—human and canine.

The best way to accustom your puppy to travelling in the car is by doing it gradually. Start with putting the puppy in the crate while you sit behind the steering wheel. Talk to him and tell him how much he will enjoy this. Repeat this the next day and start the car, letting the engine run for a couple of minutes. On the next day, drive around the block and slowly extend your trips each day. Drive to the park, let him have a quick run and feed him when you come home. Whatever you do, make it fun for him.

For long trips, be prepared to stop to let the dog relieve himself. Bring along whatever you need to clean up after him. You should bring along some

DID YOU KNOW?

When travelling, never let your dog off-lead in a strange area. Your dog could run away out of fear or decide to chase a passing squirrel or cat or simply want to stretch his legs without restriction—you might never see your canine friend again.

old towels and rags should he have an accident in the car or, despite your preparations, become carsick.

BOARDING

So you want to take a family holiday—and you want to include all members of your family.

DID YOU KNOW?

If you are going on a long car trip with your dog, be sure the hotels are dog friendly. Many hotels do not accept dogs. Also take along some ice that can be thawed and offered to your dog if he becomes overheated. Most dogs like to lick ice.

You would probably make arrangements for accommodations ahead of time anyway, but this is especially important when travelling with a dog. You do not want to make an overnight stop at the only place around for miles to find out that they do not allow dogs. Also, you do not want to reserve a place for your family without mentioning that you are bringing a dog, because if it is against their policy you may not have a place to stay.

Alternatively, if you are travelling and choose not to bring your Cocker, you will have to make arrangements for him while you are away. Some options are to bring him to a neighbour's house to stay while you are away, to have a trusted neighbour stop by often or

IDENTIFICATION

Your Cocker is your valued companion and friend. That is why you always keep a close eye on him and you have made sure that he cannot escape from the garden or wriggle out of his collar and run away from you. However, accidents can happen and there may come a time when your dog unexpectedly gets separated from you. If this unfortunate event should

Oftentimes boarding kennels are able to wash, groom and serve the health needs of your Cocker while you are away on holiday.

stay at your house, or to bring your dog to a reputable boarding kennel. If you choose to board him at a kennel, you should stop by to see the facility and where the dogs are kept to make sure that it is clean. Talk to the owner or the manager and see how he or she treats the dogs—does the staff spend time with the dogs, play with them, exercise them, etc.? You know that your Cocker will not be happy unless he gets regular activity. Also find out the kennel's policy on vaccinations and what they require. This is for all of the dogs' safety, since when dogs are kept together there is a greater risk of diseases being passed from dog to dog.

DID YOU KNOW?

If your dog gets lost, he is not able to ask for directions home.

Identification tags fastened to the collar give important information—the dog's name, the owner's name, the owner's address and a telephone number where the owner can be reached. This makes it easy for whoever finds the dog to contact the owner and arrange to have the dog returned. An added advantage is that a person will be more likely to approach a lost dog who has ID tags on his collar; it tells the person that this is somebody's pet rather than a stray. This is the easiest and fastest method of identification provided that the tags stay on the collar and the collar stays on the dog.

85

DID YOU KNOW?

As Cocker Spaniel puppies become more and more expensive, especially those puppies of high quality for showing and/or breeding, they have a greater chance of being stolen. The usual collar dog tag is, of course, easily removed. But there are two techniques which are becoming widely utilised for identification.

The puppy microchip implantation involves the injection of a small microchip, about the size of a corn kernel, under the skin of the dog. If your dog shows up at a clinic or shelter, or is offered for resale under less than savoury circumstances, it can be positively identified by the microchip. The microchip is scanned and a registry quickly identifies you as the owner. This is not only protection against theft, but should the dog run away or go chasing a squirrel and get lost, you have a fair chance of getting it back.

Tattooing is done on various parts of the dog, from its belly to its cheeks. The number tattooed can be your telephone number or any other number which you can easily memorise. When professional dog thieves see a tattooed dog, they usually lose interest in it. Both microchipping and tattooing can be done at your local veterinary clinic. For the safety of our Cocker Spaniels, no laboratory facility or dog broker will accept a tattooed dog as stock.

occur, the first thing on your mind will be finding him. Proper identification will increase the chances of his being returned to you safely and quickly. In many countries tattooing or micro-chipping the puppies before they leave the breeder is common practice and often done by the Kennel Club so that the number that is given to the puppy, either as an earmark or via the microchip, is a unique number that is also recorded on his pedigree.

Your Cocker should be tattooed for safety's sake. The tattoo could be on the inside of the thigh. (Photo retouched for clarity.)

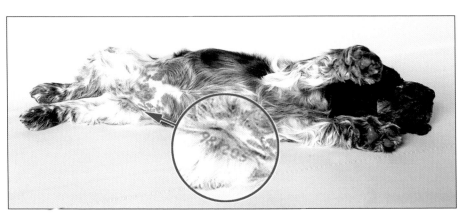

Training Your Cocker Spaniel

Living with an untrained dog is a lot like owning a piano that you do not know how to play—it is a nice object to look at but it does not do much more than that to bring you pleasure. Now try taking piano lessons and suddenly the piano comes alive and brings forth magical sounds and rhythms that set your heart singing and your body swaying.

The same is true with your Cocker. At first you enjoy seeing him around the house. He does not do much with you other than to need food, water and exercise. Come to think of it, he is a big responsibility and a lot of work. And often, he develops unacceptable behaviours that annoy and/or infuriate you, to say nothing of bad habits that may end up costing you great sums of money. Not a good thing!

Now enrol him in an obedience class. Teach him good manners as you learn how and why he behaves the way he does. Find out how to communicate with your dog and how to recognise and understand his communications with you. Suddenly the dog takes on a new role in your life—he is smart, interesting, well behaved and fun to be with, and he demonstrates his bond of devotion to you daily. In other words, your dog does wonders for your ego because he constantly reminds you that you are not only his leader, you are

There is no better investment of your time than to train your pet Cocker. A few hours spent when the Cocker is a puppy can reap rewards for many years to come.

his hero! Miraculous things have happened—you have a wonderful dog (even your family and friends have noticed the transformation!) and you feel good about yourself.

Those involved with teaching dog obedience and counselling owners about their dogs' behaviour have discovered some

Puppies are naturally curious, inquisitive and exuberant.

interesting facts about dog ownership. For example, training dogs when they are puppies results in the highest rate of success in developing well-mannered and well-adjusted adult dogs. Training an older dog, say from six months to six years of age, can produce almost equal results providing that the owner accepts the dog's slower rate of learning capability and is willing to work patiently to help the dog succeed at developing to his fullest potential. Unfortunately, the patience factor is what many owners of untrained adult dogs lack, so they do not persist until their dogs are successful at learning particular behaviours.

Training a puppy, for example, aged 10 to 16 weeks (20 weeks at the most) is like working with a dry sponge in a pool of water. The pup soaks up whatever you show him and constantly looks for more things to do and learn. At this early age, his body is not yet producing hormones, and therein lies the reason for such a high rate of success. Without hormones, he is focused on his owners and not particular-

ly interested in investigating other places, dogs, people, etc. You are his leader; his provider of food, water, shelter and security. Therefore, he latches onto you and wants to stay close. He will usually follow you from room to room, will not let you out of his sight when you are outdoors with him and will respond in like manner to the people and animals you encounter. If, for example, you greet a friend warmly, he will be happy to greet the person as well. If, however, you are hesitant, even anxious, about the approach of a stranger, he will respond accordingly.

Once the puppy begins to produce hormones, his natural curiosity emerges and he begins to investigate the world around him. It is at that time when you may notice that the untrained dog begins to wander away from you and even ignore your commands to stay

DID YOU KNOW?
Taking your dog to an obedience school may be the best investment in time and money you can ever make. You will enjoy the benefits for the lifetime of your dog and you will have the opportunity to meet people with your own behavioural criteria.

close. When this behaviour becomes a problem, the owner has two choices: get rid of the dog or train him. It is strongly urged that you choose the latter option.

Occasionally there are no classes available within a reasonable distance from the owner's home. Sometimes there are classes available but the tuition is too costly. Whatever the circumstances, the solution to the problem of lack of lesson availability lies within the pages of this book.

This chapter is devoted to helping you train your Cocker Spaniel at home. If the recommended procedures are followed faithfully, you may expect positive results that will prove rewarding to both you and your dog.

Whether your Cocker is a puppy or a mature adult, the methods of teaching and the techniques we use in training basic behaviours are the same. After all, no dog, whether puppy or adult, likes harsh or inhumane methods. All creatures, however, respond favourably to gentle motivational methods and sincere praise and encouragement. Now let us get started.

HOUSE-TRAINING

You can train a puppy to relieve himself wherever you choose. For example, city dwellers often train their puppies to relieve

themselves in the gutter because large plots of grass are not readily available. Suburbanites, on the other hand, usually have gardens to accommodate their dogs' needs. Outdoor training includes such surfaces as grass, dirt and cement. Indoor training usually means

DID YOU KNOW?
Dogs do not understand our language. They can be trained to react to a certain sound, at a certain volume. If you say 'No, Oliver' in a very soft pleasant voice it will not have the same meaning as 'No, Oliver!!' when you shout it as loud as you can. You should never use the dog's name during a reprimand, just the command NO!! Since dogs don't understand words, comics use dogs trained with opposite meanings to the world. Thus, when the comic commands his dog to SIT the dog will stand up; and vice versa.

training your dog to newspaper.

When deciding on the surface and location that you will want your puppy to use, be sure it is going to be permanent. Training your dog to grass and then changing your mind two months later is extremely difficult for both dog and owner.

Next, choose the command you will use each and every time you want your puppy to void. 'Go

DID YOU KNOW?
Never line your pup's sleeping area with newspaper. Puppy litters are usually raised on newspaper and, once in your home, the puppy will immediately associate newspaper with voiding. Never put newspaper on any floor while housetraining, as this will only confuse the puppy. If you are paper-training him, use paper in his designated relief area ONLY. Finally, restrict water intake after evening meals. Offer a few licks at a time— never let a young puppy gulp water after meals.

hurry up' and 'Go make' are examples of commands commonly used by dog owners.

Get in the habit of asking the puppy, 'Do you want to go hurry up?' (or whatever your chosen relief command is) before you take him out. That way, when he becomes an adult, you will be able to determine if he wants to go out when you ask him. A confirmation will be signs of interest, wagging his tail, watching you intently, going to the door, etc.

Puppy needs to relieve himself after play periods, after each meal, after he has been sleeping and any time he indicates that he is looking for a place to urinate or defecate. The urinary and intestinal tract muscles of very young puppies are not fully developed. Therefore,

like human babies, puppies need to relieve themselves frequently.

Take your puppy out often— every hour for an eight-week-old, for example. The older the puppy, the less often he will need to relieve himself. Finally, as a mature healthy adult, he will require only three to five relief trips per day.

HOUSING
Since the type of housing and control you provide for your puppy has a direct relationship on the success of housetraining, we consider the various aspects of both before we begin training.

Bringing a new puppy home and turning him loose in your house can be compared to turning a child loose in a sports arena and telling the child that the place is all his! The sheer enormity of the place would be too much for him to handle.

DID YOU KNOW?
Do not carry your dog to his toilet area. Lead him there on a lead or, better yet, encourage him to follow you to the spot. If you start carrying him to his spot, you might end up doing this routine forever and your dog will have the satisfaction of having trained YOU.

HOW MANY TIMES A DAY?

AGE	RELIEF TRIPS
To 14 weeks	10
14–22 weeks	8
22–32 weeks	6
Adulthood (dog stops growing)	4

These are estimates, of course, but they are a guide as to the MINIMUM opportunities a dog should have each day to relieve itself.

Instead, offer the puppy clearly defined areas where he can play, sleep, eat and live. A room of the house where the family gathers is the most obvious choice. Puppies are social animals and need to feel a part of the pack right from the start. Hearing your voice, watching you while you are doing things and smelling you nearby are all positive reinforcers that he is now a member of your pack. Usually a family room, the kitchen or a nearby adjoining breakfast nook is ideal for providing safety and security for both puppy and owner.

Within that room there should be a smaller area which the puppy can call his own. A cubbyhole, a wire or fibreglass dog crate or a fenced (not boarded!) corner from which he can view the activities of his new family will be fine. The size of the area or crate is the key factor here. The area must be large enough for the puppy to lay down and stretch out as well as stand up without rubbing his head on the top, yet small enough so that he cannot relieve himself at one end and sleep at the other without coming into contact with his droppings.

Dogs are, by nature, clean animals and will not remain close to their relief areas unless forced to do so. In those cases, they then become dirty dogs and usually remain that way for life.

The crate or cubby should be lined with a clean towel and offer one toy, no more. Do not put food or water in the crate, as eating and drinking will activate his digestive processes and ultimately defeat your purpose as well as make the puppy very uncomfortable as he attempts to 'hold it.'

DID YOU KNOW?

If you start with a normal, healthy dog and give him time, patience and some carefully executed lessons, you will reap the rewards of that training for the life of the dog. And what a life it will be! The two of you will find immeasurable pleasure in the companionship you have built together with love, respect and understanding. Good luck and enjoy!

Be prepared for your puppy's arrival. Ask your breeder to recommend the equipment that you will need.

DID YOU KNOW?

By providing sleeping and resting quarters that fit the dog, and offering frequent opportunities to relieve himself outside his quarters, the puppy quickly learns that the outdoors (or the newspaper if you are training him to paper) is the place to go when he needs to urinate or defecate. It also reinforces his innate desire to keep his sleeping quarters clean. This, in turn, helps develop the muscle control that will eventually produce a dog with clean living habits.

THE SUCCESS METHOD
6 Steps to Successful Crate Training

1 Tell the puppy 'Crate time!' and place him in the crate with a small treat (a piece of cheese or half of a biscuit). Let him stay in the crate for five minutes while you are in the same room. Then release him and praise lavishly. Never release him when he is fussing. Wait until he is quiet before you let him out.

2 Repeat Step 1 several times a day.

3 The next day, place the puppy in the crate as before. Let him stay there for ten minutes. Do this several times.

4 Continue building time in five-minute increments until the puppy stays in his crate for 30 minutes with you in the room. Always take him to his relief area after prolonged periods in his crate.

5 Now go back to Step 1 and let the puppy stay in his crate for five minutes, this time while you are out of the room.

6 Once again, build crate time in five-minute increments with you out of the room. When the puppy will stay willingly in his crate (he may even fall asleep!) for 30 minutes with you out of the room, he will be ready to stay in it for several hours at a time.

Canine Development Schedule

It is important to understand how and at what age a puppy develops into adulthood. If you are a puppy owner, consult the following Canine Development Schedule to determine the stage of development your Cocker Spaniel puppy is currently experiencing. This knowledge will help you as you work with the puppy in the weeks and months ahead.

Period	Age	Characteristics
First to Third	**Birth to Seven Weeks**	Puppy needs food, sleep and warmth, and responds to simple and gentle touching. Needs mother for security and disciplining. Needs litter mates for learning and interacting with other dogs. Pup learns to function within a pack and learns pack order of dominance. Begin socialising with adults and children for short periods. Begins to become aware of its environment.
Fourth	**Eight to Twelve Weeks**	Brain is fully developed. Needs socialising with outside world. Remove from mother and littermates. Needs to change from canine pack to human pack. Human dominance necessary. Fear period occurs between 8 and 16 weeks. Avoid fright and pain.
Fifth	**Thirteen to Sixteen Weeks**	Training and formal obedience should begin. Less association with other dogs, more with people, places, situations. Period will pass easily if you remember this is pup's change-to-adolescence time. Be firm and fair. Flight instinct prominent. Permissiveness and over-disciplining can do permanent damage. Praise for good behaviour.
Juvenile	**Four to Eight Months**	Another fear period about 7 to 8 months of age. It passes quickly, but be cautious of fright and pain. Sexual maturity reached. Dominant traits established. Dog should understand sit, down, come and stay by now.

Note: These are approximate time frames. Allow for individual differences in puppies.

CONTROL

By control, we mean helping the puppy to create a lifestyle pattern that will be compatible to that of his human pack (YOU!). Just as we guide little children to learn our way of life, we must show the puppy when it is time to play, eat, sleep, exercise and even entertain himself.

Your puppy should always sleep in his crate. He should also learn that, during times of household confusion and excessive human activity (such as at breakfast when family members are preparing for the day), he can play by himself in relative safety and comfort in his crate. Each time you leave the puppy alone, he should be crated. Puppies are chewers. They cannot tell the difference between lamp cables, television wires, shoes, table legs, etc. Chewing into a television wire, for example, can be fatal to the puppy while a shorted wire can start a fire in the house.

If the puppy chews on the arm of the chair when he is alone, you will probably discipline him angrily when you get home. Thus, he makes the association that your coming home means he is going to be punished. (He will not remember chewing up the chair and is incapable of making the association of the discipline with his naughty deed.)

Other times of excitement, such as family parties, etc., can be fun for the puppy providing he can view the activities from the security of his crate. He is not underfoot and he is not being fed all sorts of titbits that will probably cause him stomach distress, yet he still feels a part of the fun.

SCHEDULE

As stated earlier, a puppy should be taken to his relief area each time he is released from his crate, after meals, after a play session, when he first awakens in the morning (at age 8 weeks, this can mean 5 a.m.!) and whenever he indicates by circling or sniffing busily that he needs to urinate or defecate. For a puppy less than ten weeks of age, a routine of taking him out every hour is necessary. As the puppy grows, he will be able to wait for longer periods of time.

Keep trips to his relief area short. Stay no more than five or six minutes and then return to the house. If he goes during that time, praise him lavishly and take him indoors immediately. If he does not, but he has an accident when you go back indoors, pick him up immediately, say 'No! No!' and return to his relief area. Wait a few minutes, then return to the house again. NEVER hit a puppy or rub his face in urine or excrement when he has an accident!

Once indoors, put the puppy in his crate until you have had

DID YOU KNOW?
Dogs are the most honourable animals in existence. They consider another species (humans) as their own. They interface with you. You are their leader. Puppies perceive children to be on their level: their actions around small children are different than their behaviour around their adult masters.

time to clean up his accident. Then release him to the family area and watch him more closely than before. Chances are, his accident was a result of your not picking up his signal or waiting too long before offering him the opportunity to relieve himself. NEVER hold a grudge against the puppy for accidents.

Let the puppy learn that going outdoors means it is time to relieve himself, not play. Once trained, he will be able to play indoors and out and still differentiate between the times for play versus the times for relief.

Help him develop regular hours for naps, being alone, playing by himself and just resting, all in his crate. Encourage him to entertain himself while you are busy with your activities. Let him learn that having you near is comforting, but it is not your main purpose in life to provide him with undivided attention.

DID YOU KNOW?
Dogs will do anything for your attention. If you reward the dog when he is calm and resting, you will develop a well-mannered dog. If, on the other hand, you greet your dog excitedly and encourage him to wrestle and roughhouse with you, the dog will greet you the same way and you will have a hyper dog on your hands.

will need to have a place where your dog can stay and be happy and safe. Crate training is the answer for now and in the future.

In conclusion, a few key elements are really all you need for a successful house and crate training method—consistency, frequency, praise, control and supervision. By following these procedures with a normal, healthy puppy, you and the puppy will soon be past the stage of 'accidents' and ready to move on to a full and rewarding life together.

Each time you put a puppy in his crate tell him, 'Crate time!' (or whatever command you choose). Soon, he will run to his crate when he hears you say those words.

In the beginning of his training, do not leave him in his crate for prolonged periods of time except during the night when everyone is sleeping. Make his experience with his crate a pleasant one and, as an adult, he will love his crate and willingly stay in it for a couple of hours.

Crate training provides safety for you, the puppy and the home. It also provides the puppy with a feeling of security, and that helps the puppy achieve self-confidence and clean habits.

Remember that one of the primary ingredients in housetraining your puppy is control. Regardless of your lifestyle, there will always be occasions when you

ROLES OF DISCIPLINE, REWARD AND PUNISHMENT

Discipline, training one to act in accordance with rules, brings order to life. It is as simple as that. Without discipline, particularly in a group society, chaos reigns supreme

DID YOU KNOW?

Dogs are sensitive to their master's moods and emotions. Use your voice wisely when communicating with your dog. Never raise your voice at your dog unless you are angry and trying to correct him. 'Barking' at your dog can become as meaningless as 'dogspeak' is to you. Think before you bark!

and the group will eventually perish. Humans and canines are social animals and need some form of discipline in order to function effectively. They must procure food, protect their home base and their young and reproduce to keep the species going. If there were no discipline in the lives of social animals, they would eventually die from starvation and/or predation by other stronger animals.

In the case of domestic canines, dogs need discipline in their lives in order to understand how their pack (you and other family members) functions and how they must act in order to survive.

A large humane society in a highly populated area surveyed dog owners regarding their satisfaction with their relationships with their dogs. People who had trained their dogs were 75% more satisfied with their pets than those who had never trained their dogs.

Dr. Edward Thorndike, a psychologist, established *Thorndike's Theory of Learning*, which states that a behaviour that results in a pleasant event tends to be repeated. A behaviour that results in an unpleasant event tends not to be repeated. It is this theory on which training methods are based today. For example, if you manipulate a dog to perform a specific behaviour and reward

him for doing it, he is likely to do it again because he enjoyed the end result.

Occasionally, punishment, a penalty inflicted for an offence, is necessary. The best type of punishment often comes from an

Discipline is necessary to train a dog to behave in a predictable manner. Believe it or not, your dog will respect you more if you discipline him. Dogs respect authority.

outside source. For example, a child is told not to touch the stove because he may get burned. He disobeys and touches the stove. In doing so, he receives a burn. From that time on, he respects the heat of the stove and avoids contact with it. Therefore, a behaviour that results in an unpleasant event tends not to be repeated.

A good example of a dog learning the hard way is the dog

97

CHOOSE THE PROPER COLLAR

The buckle collar is the standard collar used for everyday purpose. Be sure that you adjust the buckle on growing puppies. Check it every day. It can become too tight overnight! These collars can be made of leather or nylon. Attach your dog's identification tags to this collar.

The halter is for a trained dog that has to be restrained to prevent running away, chasing a cat and the like. Considered the most humane of all collars, it is frequently used on smaller dogs for which collars are not comfortable.

who chases the house cat. He is told many times to leave the cat alone, yet he persists in teasing the cat. Then, one day he begins chasing the cat but the cat turns and swipes a claw across the dog's face, leaving him with a painful gash on his nose. The final result is that the dog stops chasing the cat.

TRAINING EQUIPMENT
COLLAR
A simple buckle collar is fine for most dogs. One who pulls mightily on the lead may require a harness.

LEAD
A 1- to 2-metre lead is recommended, preferably made of leather, nylon or heavy cloth. A chain lead is not recommended, as many dog owners find that the chain cuts into their hands and that switching the lead back and forth frequently between their hands is painful.

TREATS
Have a bag of treats on hand. Something nutritious and easy to swallow works best; use a soft treat, a chunk of cheese or a piece of cooked chicken rather than a dry biscuit. By the time the dog gets done chewing a dry treat, he will forget why he is being rewarded in the first place! Using food rewards will not teach a dog to beg at the table—the only way to teach a dog to beg at the table is

to give him food from the table. In training, rewarding the dog with a food treat away from the table will help him associate praise and the treats with learning new behaviours that obviously please his owner.

TRAINING BEGINS: ASK THE DOG A QUESTION

In order to teach your dog anything, you must first get his attention. After all, he cannot learn anything if he is looking away from you with his mind on something else.

To get his attention, ask him, 'School?' and immediately walk over to him and give him a treat as you tell him 'Good dog.' Wait a minute or two and repeat the routine, this time with a treat in your hand as you approach the dog to within a foot of him. Do not go directly to him, but stop about a foot short of him and hold out the treat as you ask, 'School?' He will see you approaching with a treat in your hand and most likely begin walking toward you. As you meet, give him the treat and praise again.

The third time, ask the question, have a treat in your hand and walk only a short distance toward the dog so that he must walk almost all the way to you. As he reaches you, give him the treat and praise again.

By this time, the dog will probably be getting the idea that if

he pays attention to you, especially when you ask that question, it will pay off in treats and fun activities for him. In other words, he learns that 'school' means doing fun things with you that result in treats and positive attention for him.

Remember that the dog does not understand your verbal language, he only recognises sounds. Your question translates to a series of sounds for him, and

> ### DID YOU KNOW?
> If you want to be successful in training your dog, you have four rules to obey yourself:
> 1. Develop an understanding of how a dog thinks.
> 2. Do not blame the dog for lack of communication.
> 3. Define your dog's personality and act accordingly.
> 4. Have patience and be consistent.

those sounds become the signal to go to you and pay attention; if he does, he will get to interact with you plus receive treats and praise.

THE BASIC COMMANDS
TEACHING SIT
Now that you have the dog's attention, hold the lead in your left hand and the food treat in your right. Place your food hand at the dog's nose and let him lick the treat but not take it from you. Say 'Sit' and slowly raise your food hand

If your Cocker doesn't make eye contact with you during training, you won't have much chance for immediate success.

of the food treats but still maintain the verbal praise. After all, you will always have your voice with you, but there will be many times when you have no food rewards yet you expect the dog to obey.

TEACHING DOWN
Teaching the down exercise is easy when you understand how the dog perceives the down position, and it is very difficult when you do not. In addition, teaching the down exercise using the wrong method can sometimes make the dog develop such a fear of the down that he either runs away when you say 'Down' or he will simply refuse to do so.

Have the dog sit close alongside

from in front of the dog's nose up over his head so that he is looking at the ceiling. As he bends his head upward, he will have to bend his knees to maintain his balance. As he bends his knees, he will assume a sit position. At that point, release the food treat and praise lavishly with comments such as 'Good dog! Good sit!', etc. Remember to always praise enthusiastically because dogs relish verbal praise from their owners and feel so proud of themselves whenever they accomplish a behaviour.

You will not use food forever in getting the dog to obey your commands. Food is only used to teach new behaviours, and once the dog knows what you want when you give a specific command, you will wean him off

DID YOU KNOW?
The puppy should also have regular play and exercise sessions when he is with you or a family member. Exercise for a very young puppy can consist of a short walk around the house or garden. Playing can include fetching games with a large ball or an old sock with a knot tied in the middle. (All puppies teethe and need soft things upon which to chew.) Remember to restrict play periods to indoors within his living area (the family room for example) until he is completely housetrained.

your left leg, facing in the same direction as you are. Hold the lead in your left hand and a food treat in your right. Now place your left hand lightly on the top of the dog's shoulders where they meet above the spinal cord. Do not push down on the dog's shoulders; simply rest your left hand there so you can guide the dog to lie down close to your left leg rather than to swing away from your side when he drops.

Now place the food hand at the dog's nose, say 'Down' very softly (almost a whisper), and slowly lower the food hand to the dog's front feet. When the food hand reaches the floor, begin moving it forward along the floor in front of the dog. Keep talking softly to the dog, saying things like, 'Do you want this treat? You can do this, good dog.' Your reassuring tone of voice will help calm the dog as

DID YOU KNOW?
The golden rule of dog training is simple. For each 'question' (command), there is only one correct answer (reaction). One command = one reaction. Keep practising the command until the dog reacts correctly without hesitating. Be repetitive but not monotonous. Dogs get bored just as people do!

DID YOU KNOW?
Practice Makes Perfect!
• Have training lessons with your dog every day in several short segments—three to five times a day for a few minutes at a time is ideal.
• Do not have long practice sessions. The dog will become easily bored.
• Never practice when you are tired, ill, worried or in an otherwise negative mood. This will transmit to the dog and may have an adverse effect on its performance.

Think fun, short and above all POSITIVE! End each session on a high note, rather than a failed exercise, and make sure to give a lot of praise. Enjoy the training and help your dog enjoy it, too.

he tries to follow the food hand in order to get the treat.

When the dog's elbows touch the floor, release the food and praise softly. Try to get the dog to maintain

When your Cocker puppy goes down on command, make him feel comfortable and rewarded in the down position.

that down position for several seconds before you let him sit up again. The goal here is to get the dog to settle down and not feel threatened in the down position.

Training to sit/stay is an absolute necessity for a field dog.

TEACHING STAY

It is easy to teach the dog to stay in either a sit or a down position. Again, we use food and praise during the teaching process as we help the dog to understand exactly what it is that we are expecting him to do.

To teach the sit/stay, start

DID YOU KNOW?

Training a dog is a life experience. Many parents admit that much of what they know about raising children they learned from caring for their dogs. Dogs respond to love, fairness and guidance, just as children do. Become a good dog owner and you may become an even better parent.

with the dog sitting on your left side as before and hold the lead in your left hand. Have a food treat in your right hand and place your food hand at the dog's nose. Say 'Stay' and step out on your right foot to stand directly in front of the dog, toe to toe, as he licks and nibbles the treat. Be sure to keep his head facing upward to maintain the sit position. Count to five and then swing around to stand next to the dog again with him on your left. As soon as you get back to the original position, release the food and praise lavishly.

To teach the down/stay, do the down as previously described. As soon as the dog lies down, say 'Stay' and step out on your right foot just as you did in the sit/stay. Count to five and then return to stand beside the dog with him on your left side. Release the treat and praise as always.

Within a week or ten days, you can begin to add a bit of distance between you and your dog when you leave him. When you do, use your left hand open with the palm facing the dog as a stay signal, much the same as the hand signal a police officer uses to stop traffic at an intersection. Hold the food treat in your right hand as before, but this time the food is not touching the dog's nose. He will watch the food hand and quickly learn that he is going to get that treat as soon as you return to his side.

When you can stand 1 metre away from your dog for 30 seconds, you can then begin building time and distance in both stays. Eventually, the dog can be expected to remain in the stay position for prolonged periods of time until you return to him or call him to you. Always praise lavishly when he stays.

TEACHING COME

If you make teaching 'Come' a fun experience, you should never have a 'student' that does not love the game or that fails to come when called. The secret, it seems, is never to teach the word 'Come.'

At times when an owner most wants his dog to come when called, the owner is likely upset or anxious and he allows these

> **DID YOU KNOW?**
> Most of all, be consistent. Always take your dog to the same location, always use the same command, and always have him on lead when he is in his relief area, unless a fenced-in garden is available.
>
> By following the Success Method, your Cocker Spaniel puppy will be completely housetrained by the time his muscle and brain development reach maturity. Keep in mind that small breeds usually mature faster than large breeds, but all puppies should be trained by six months of age.

feelings to come through in the tone of his voice when he calls his dog. Hearing that desperation in his owner's voice, the dog fears the results of going to him and therefore either disobeys outright or runs in the opposite direction. The secret, therefore, is to teach the dog a game and, when you want him to come to you, simply play the game. It is practically a no-fail solution!

To begin, have several members of your family take a few food treats and each go into a different room in the house. Take turns calling the dog, and each person should celebrate the dog's finding him with a treat and lots of happy praise. When a person calls the dog, he is actually

A treat and much praise are rewards for a job well done.

inviting the dog to find him and get a treat as a reward for 'winning.'

A few turns of the 'Where are you?' game and the dog will figure out that everyone is playing the game and that each person has a big celebration awaiting his success at locating them. Once he learns to love the game, simply calling out 'Where are you?' will bring him running from wherever he is when he hears that all-important question.

The come command is recognised as one of the most important things to teach a dog, so it is interesting to note that there are trainers who work with thousands of dogs and never teach the actual word 'Come.' Yet these dogs will race to respond to a person who uses the dog's name followed by 'Where are you?' In one instance, for example, a woman has a 12-year-old compan-ion dog who went blind, but who

DID YOU KNOW?

A basic obedience beginner's class usually lasts for six to eight weeks. Dog and owner attend an hour-long lesson once a week and practice for a few minutes, several times a day, each day at home. If done properly, the whole procedure will result in a well-mannered dog and an owner who delights in living with a pet that is eager to please and enjoys doing things with his owner.

never fails to locate her owner when asked, 'Where are you?'

Children particularly love to play this game with their dogs. Children can hide in smaller places like a shower stall or bathtub, behind a bed or under a table. The dog needs to work a little bit harder to find these hiding places, but when he does he loves to celebrate with a treat and a tussle with a favourite youngster.

TEACHING HEEL

Heeling means that the dog walks beside the owner without pulling. It takes time and patience on the owner's part to succeed at teaching the dog that he (the owner) will not proceed unless the dog is walking calmly beside him. Pulling out ahead on the lead is definitely not acceptable.

Begin by holding the lead in your left hand as the dog sits

DID YOU KNOW?

When calling the dog, do not say 'Come.' Say things like, 'Rover, where are you? See if you can find me! I have a biscuit for you!' Keep up a constant line of chatter with coaxing sounds and frequent questions such as, 'Where are you?' The dog will learn to follow the sound of your voice to locate you and receive his reward.

beside your left leg. Hold the loop end of the lead in your right hand but keep your left hand short on the lead so it keeps the dog in close next to you.

Say 'Heel' and step forward on your left foot. Keep the dog close to you and take three steps. Stop and have the dog sit next to you in what we now call the 'heel position.' Praise verbally, but do not touch the dog. Hesitate a moment and begin again with 'Heel,' taking three steps and stopping, at which point the dog is told to sit again.

Your goal here is to have the dog walk those three steps without pulling on the lead. When he will walk calmly beside you for three steps without pulling, increase the number of steps you take to five. When he will walk politely beside you while you take five steps, you can increase the length of your walk to ten steps. Keep increasing the length

DID YOU KNOW?
Teach your dog to HEEL in an enclosed area. Once you think the dog will obey reliably and you want to attempt advanced obedience exercises such as off-lead heeling, test him in a fenced in area so he cannot run away.

of your stroll until the dog will walk quietly beside you without pulling as long as you want him to heel. When you stop heeling, indicate to the dog that the exercise is over by verbally

DID YOU KNOW?
If you begin teaching the heel by taking long walks and letting the dog pull you along, he misinterprets this action as an acceptable form of taking a walk. When you pull back on the lead to counteract his pulling, he reads that tug as a signal to pull even harder!

praising as you pet him and say 'OK, good dog.' The 'OK' is used as a release word meaning that the exercise is finished and the dog is free to relax.

If you are dealing with a dog who insists on pulling you around, simply 'put on your brakes' and stand your ground until the dog realises that the two of you are not going anywhere until he is beside you and moving at your pace, not his. It may take some time just standing there to convince the dog that you are the leader and you will be the one to decide on the direction and speed of your travel.

Each time the dog looks up at you or slows down to give a slack lead between the two of you,

DID YOU KNOW?

A dog in jeopardy never lies down. He stays alert on his feet because instinct tells him that he may have to run away or fight for his survival. Therefore, if a dog feels threatened or anxious, he will not lie down. Consequently, it is important to have the dog calm and relaxed as he learns the down exercise.

quietly praise him and say, 'Good heel. Good dog.' Eventually, the dog will begin to respond and within a few days he will be walking politely beside you without pulling on the lead. At first, the training sessions should be kept short and very positive; soon the dog will be able to walk nicely with you for increasingly longer distances. Remember also to give the dog free time and the opportunity to run and play when you are done with heel practice.

WEANING OFF FOOD IN TRAINING

Food is used in training new behaviours, yet once the dog understands what behaviour goes with a specific command, it is time to start weaning him off the food treats. At first, give a treat after each exercise. Then, start to give a treat only after every other exercise. Mix up the times when you offer a food reward and the times when you only offer praise so that the dog will never know when he is going to receive both food and praise and when he is going to receive only praise. This is called a variable ratio reward system and it proves successful because there is always the chance that the owner will produce a treat, so the dog never stops trying for that reward. No matter what, ALWAYS give verbal praise.

OBEDIENCE CLASSES

As previously discussed, it is a good idea to enrol in an obedience class if one is available in your area. Many areas have dog clubs that offer basic obedience training as well as preparatory classes for obedience competition.

At obedience trials, dogs can earn titles at various levels of competition. The beginning levels of competition include basic behaviours such as sit, down, heel, etc. The more advanced levels of competition include

Many successful show dogs, if not most, are trained to the stand position by using food rewards as incentives.

more or less the same commands but more complex, such as staying while you disappear out of sight, heel without a lead etc. The commands the dogs learn are extremely useful and the training classes are great fun for you and your dog.

GUNDOG TRAINING

The Spaniels' duties in the field consist of working close to the sportsman to quest for game, flush it and retrieve it when called upon to do so. If you want to train to Cocker Spaniel for work, you have to start the pup at an early age. The basis for every training is obedience and that is where you start with your puppy right away. Basic commands such as 'come,' 'sit' and 'heel' can be taught to the puppy, and everything he learns when he is still under 6 months

If your Cocker has his own chew toys, he should leave your knitting alone!

DID YOU KNOW?

To a dog's way of thinking, your hands are like his mouth in terms of a defence mechanism. If you squeeze him too tightly, he might just bite you because that would be his normal response. This is not aggressive biting and, although all biting should be discouraged, you need the discipline in learning how to handle your dog.

old will not be forgotten. You can also start to teach him to retrieve a small object or dummy. This can be a sock or a rabbit skin or a wing of a bird. If you throw the object a few yards ahead of your puppy, he will run to it and pick it up. Call him by his name and encourage him to bring it back to you. Do not be discouraged if your puppy thinks this is lovely game and runs off with the object! If he does that, move away from him, calling him by his name. Always remember to reward him whenever possible.

A Cocker is usually an excellent retriever and swimmer. Test these skills in shallow waters. Once you are convinced of his ability to swim (especially when there is a current), you can throw floatable toys into the water and train him to bring them to you. With a little encouragement, your Cocker will swim out, retrieve the object and then bring it back to where you are waiting.

The next lesson is to encourage him to use his nose. By dragging a piece of tripe you can make a trail for him to work out. You can also throw the dummy into light cover, where it is out of sight, and encourage your Cocker to locate and then to retrieve it. You must be very careful with the puppy when he starts teething because picking up the dummy might be quite painful and forcing him to pick it up would do irreparable harm to his willingness to retrieve. By the time your puppy is eight or nine months old, knows his basic obedience and has learned to retrieve and use his nose, you can join a training class. Depending on his natural aptitude, you can train him for competition in working tests and field trials.

OTHER ACTIVITIES FOR LIFE
Whether a dog is trained in the structured environment of a class or alone with his owner at home, there are many activities that can bring fun and rewards to both owner and dog once they have mastered basic control.

Teaching the dog to help out around the home, in the garden or on the farm provides great satisfaction to both dog and owner. In addition, the dog's help makes life a little easier for his owner and raises his stature as a valued companion to his family. It helps give the dog a purpose; it helps to keep his mind occupied and provides an outlet for his energy.

Backpacking is an exciting and healthful activity that the dog can be taught without assistance from more than his owner. The exercise of walking and climbing is good for man and dog alike, and the bond that they develop together is priceless.

If you are interested in participating in organised competition with your Cocker, there are other activities other than obedience in which you and your dog can become involved. Agility is a popular and fun sport where dogs run through an obstacle course that includes various jumps, tunnels and other exercises to test the dog's speed and coordination. The owners often run through the course beside their dogs to give

ocker Spaniel.

„Nell".
A. Leroy, Senlis.

commands and to guide them through the course. Although competitive, the focus is on fun—it's fun to do and fun to watch, as well as great exercise.

DID YOU KNOW?

Occasionally, a dog and owner who have not attended formal classes have been able to earn entry-level titles by obtaining competition rules and regulations from a local breed club and practising on their own to a degree of perfection. Obtaining the higher level titles, however, almost always requires extensive training under the tutelage of experienced instructors. In addition, the more difficult levels require more specialised equipment whereas the lower levels do not.

Illustrations from the late 1800s of the Cocker Spaniel frequently depict the breed with retrieved game, indicating its use in England 200 years ago.

Colinwood Cowboy, long deceased, was a great pheasant retriever as shown in this historic action photo.

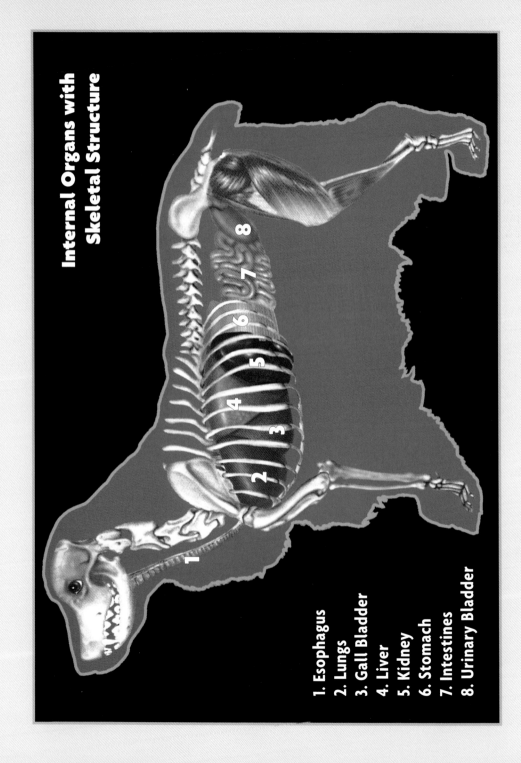

Health Care of Your Cocker Spaniel

Dogs, being mammals like human beings, suffer many of the same physical illnesses as people. They might even share many of the same psychological problems. Since people usually know more about human diseases than canine maladies, many of the terms used in this chapter will be the familiar terms, not necessarily those used by veterinary surgeons. We'll still use the term X-RAY, instead of the more acceptable term RADIOGRAPH. We will also use the familiar term SYMPTOMS; even though dogs don't have symptoms, they do have CLINICAL SIGNS. SYMPTOMS, by the way, are verbal descrip-

tions of the patient's feelings. Since dogs can't speak, we have to look for clinical signs...but we still use the term SYMPTOMS in this book.

As a general rule, medicine is PRACTISED. That term is not arbitrary. Medicine is an art. It is a constantly changing art as we learn more and more about genetics, electronic aids (like CAT scans) and opinions. There are many dog maladies, like canine hip dysplasia, which are not universally treated in the same manner. Some veterinary surgeons opt for surgery more often than others.

SELECTING A VETERINARY SURGEON

Your selection of a veterinary surgeon should not be based upon personality (as most are) but upon their convenience to your home. You want a doctor who is close as you might have emergencies or multiple visits for treatments. You want a doctor who has a good reputation for ability and responsiveness. There is nothing more frustrating than having to wait a day or more to get a response from a veterinary surgeon.

Select a reputable veterinary surgeon close to your home and don't be hesitant to discuss fees, the equipment available, his office hours, emergency telephone numbers and the like.

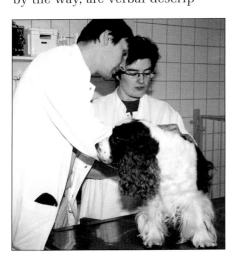

wounds. When the problem affecting your dog is serious, it is not unusual or impudent to get another medical opinion. You might also want to compare costs between several veterinary surgeons. Sophisticated health care and veterinary services can be very costly. Don't be bashful to discuss these costs with your veterinary surgeon or his (her) staff. It is not infrequent that important decisions are based upon financial considerations.

PREVENTATIVE MEDICINE

It is much easier, less costly and more effective to practise preventative medicine than to fight bouts of illness and disease. Properly bred puppies come from parents that were selected based upon their genetic disease profile. Their mothers should have been vaccinated, free of all

All veterinary surgeons are licensed and their diplomas and/or certificates should be displayed in their waiting rooms. There are, however, many veterinary specialities, which usually require further studies and internships. There are specialists in heart problems (veterinary cardiologists), skin problems (veterinary dermatologists), teeth and gum problems (veterinary dentists), eye problems (veterinary ophthalmologists) and X-rays (veterinary radiologists), as well as surgeons who have specialities in bones, muscles or other organs. Most veterinary surgeons do routine surgery such as neutering and stitching up internal and external parasites and properly nourished.

Puppies should be weaned by the time they are about two months old. A puppy that remains for at least eight weeks with its mother and littermates usually adapts better to other dogs and people later in its life.

In every case, you should have your newly acquired puppy examined by a veterinary surgeon immediately. Vaccination programmes usually begin when the puppy is very young.

The puppy will have its teeth examined, have its skeletal conformation checked and have its general health checked prior to certification by the veterinary surgeon.

DID YOU KNOW?

A dental examination is in order when the dog is between six months and one year of age and any permanent teeth that have erupted incorrectly can be corrected. It is important to begin a brushing regimen, preferably using a two-sided brushing technique, whereby both sides of the tooth are brushed at the same time. Durable nylon and safe edible chews should be a part of your puppy's arsenal for good health, good teeth and pleasant breath. The vast majority of dogs three to four years old and older has diseases of their gums from lack of dental attention. Using the various types of dental chews can be very effective in controlling dental plaque.

By the time your dog is a year old, you should have become very comfortable with your local veterinary surgeon and have agreed on scheduled visits for booster vaccinations. Blood tests should now be taken regularly, for comparative purposes, for such variables as cholesterol and triglyceride levels, thyroid hormones, liver enzymes, blood cell counts, etc.

The eyes, ears, nose and throat should be examined regularly and annual cleaning of the teeth is a ritual. For teeth scaling, the dog must be anaesthetised.

Having your dog's teeth examined should be a part of the annual routine physical examination conducted by your veterinary surgeon.

VACCINATION SCHEDULING

Most vaccinations are given by injection and should only be done by a veterinary surgeon. Both he

HEALTH AND VACCINATION SCHEDULE

Age in Weeks:	3rd	6th	8th	10th	12th	14th	16th	20-24th
Worm Control	✔	✔	✔	✔	✔	✔	✔	✔
Neutering								✔
Heartworm		✔						✔
Parvovirus		✔		✔		✔		✔
Distemper			✔		✔		✔	
Hepatitis			✔		✔		✔	
Leptospirosis		✔		✔		✔		
Parainfluenza		✔		✔		✔		
Dental Examination			✔					✔
Complete Physical			✔					✔
Temperament Testing			✔					
Coronavirus					✔			
Kennel Cough		✔						
Hip Dysplasia							✔	

Vaccinations are not instantly effective. It takes about two weeks for the dog's immunisation system to develop antibodies. Most vaccinations require annual booster shots. Your veterinary surgeon should guide you in this regard.

and you should keep a record of the date of the injection, the identification of the vaccine and the amount given. The first vaccinations should start when the puppy is 6 weeks old, then when it is 9 weeks of age and later when it is 12–14 weeks of age. Vaccinations should NEVER be given without a 15-day lapse between injections. Most vaccinations immunise your puppy against viruses.

The usual vaccines contain immunising doses of several different viruses such as distemper, parvovirus, parainfluenza and hepatitis. There are other

DID YOU KNOW?

Vaccines do not work all the time. Sometimes dogs are allergic to them and many times the antibodies, which are supposed to be stimulated by the vaccine, just are not produced. You should keep your dog in the veterinary clinic for an hour after it is vaccinated to be sure there are no allergic reactions.

vaccines available when the puppy is at risk. You should rely upon professional advice. This is especially true for the booster shot programme. Most vaccination programmes require a booster when the puppy is a year old, and once a year thereafter. In some cases, circumstances may require more frequent immunisations.

Kennel cough, more formally known as tracheobronchitis, is treated with a vaccine that is sprayed into the dog's nostrils.

The effectiveness of a parvovirus vaccination programme can be tested to be certain that the vaccinations are protective. Your veterinary

DID YOU KNOW?
Feeding your dog properly is very important. An incorrect diet could affect the dog's health, behaviour and nervous system, possibly making a normal dog into an aggressive one.

surgeon will explain and manage all of these details.

YEARLY EXAMS
Continue to visit the veterinary surgeon at least once a year throughout your dog's life for a physical exam. There is no such disease as old age, but bodily functions do change with age. The eyes and ears as well as the

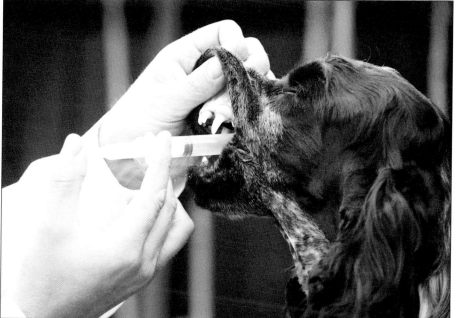

Liquid medicines can be given with a syringe. Ask your vet to demonstrate the best way to administer the medication.

MEDICAL PROBLEMS
MOST FREQUENTLY SEEN IN COCKER SPANIELS

Condition	Age Affected	Cause	Area Affected
Acral Lick Dermatitis (hot spots)	Any age, males	Unknown	Legs
Cataracts	Young	Hereditary	Eyes
Elbow Dysplasia	4 to 7 mos	Congenital	Elbow joint
Familial Nephropathy (FN)	12 weeks to 2 1/2 years	Inherited	Kidneys
Gastric Dilatation (Bloat)	Older dogs	Swallowing air	Stomach
Hip Dysplasia	By 2 years	Congenital	Hip joint
Progressive Retinal Atrophy	3 to 7 years	Hereditary	Retinal tissue/eyes
Von Willebrand's Disease	Birth	Congenital	Blood

First Aid
at a Glance

Burns
Place the affected area under cool water; use ice if only a small area is burnt.

Bee/Insect bites
Apply ice to relieve swelling; antihistamine dosed properly.

Animal bites
Clean any bleeding area; apply pressure until bleeding subsides; go to the vet.

Car accident
Move dog from roadway with blanket; seek veterinary aid.

Antifreeze poisoning
Immediately induce vomiting by using hydrogen peroxide.

Fish hooks
Removal best handled by vet; hook must be cut in order to remove.

Shock
Calm the dog, keep him warm; seek immediate veterinary help.

Nosebleed
Apply cold compress to the nose; apply pressure to any visible abrasion.

Bleeding
Apply pressure above the area; treat wound by applying a cotton pack.

Heat stroke
Submerge dog in cold bath; cool down with fresh air and water; go to the vet.

Frostbite/Hypothermia
Warm the dog with a warm bath, electric blankets or hot water bottles.

Abrasions
Clean the wound and clean out thoroughly with fresh water; apply antiseptic.

Remember: an injured dog may attempt to bite a helping hand from fear and confusion. Always muzzle the dog before trying to offer assistance.

internal workings of the liver, kidneys and intestines become less efficient with age. Follow your veterinary surgeon's advice to keep your Cocker Spaniel in good health year after year.

DID YOU KNOW?
The myth that dogs need extra fat in their diets can be harmful. Should your vet recommend extra fat, use safflower oil instead of animal oils. Safflower oil has been shown to be less likely to cause allergic reactions.

SKIN PROBLEMS IN COCKERS

Veterinary surgeons are consulted by dog owners for skin problems more than for any other group of diseases or maladies. Dogs' skin is almost as sensitive as human skin and both suffer almost the same maladies (though the occurrence of acne in dogs is rare!). For this reason, veterinary dermatology has developed into a speciality practised by many veterinary surgeons.

Since many skin problems have visual symptoms which are almost identical, it requires the skill of an experienced veterinary dermatologist to identify and cure many of the more severe skin disorders. Simply put, if your dog is suffering from a skin disorder, seek professional assistance as

quickly as possible. As with all diseases, the earlier a problem is identified and treated, the more successful is the cure.

Pet shops sell many treatments for skin problems. Most of the treatments are simply directed at symptoms and not the underlying problem(s).

PARASITE BITES
Many of us are allergic to mosquito bites. The bites itch, erupt and may even become infected. Dogs have the same reaction to fleas, ticks and/or mites. When you feel the prick of the mosquito when it bites you, you have a chance to kill it with your hand. Unfortunately, when our dog is bitten by a flea, tick or mite, it can only scratch it away or bite it. By the time the dog has been bitten, the parasite has done some of its damage. It may also have laid eggs to cause further problems in the near future.

DID YOU KNOW?
Your dog's protein needs are changeable. High activity level, stress, climate and other physical factors may require your dog to have more protein in his diet. Check with your veterinary surgeon.

The itching from parasite bites is probably due to the saliva injected into the site when the parasite sucks the dog's blood.

HOT SPOTS

Patches of skin that become irritated and inflamed, referred to by veterinary surgeons as acute moist dermatitis, are more commonly known as 'hot spots.' Long-coated breeds such as the Cocker Spaniel are especially prone to these sores, which usually result from self-trauma. Some precipitating causes include otitis (inflammation of the ear), external parasites, anal sac irritation and other epidermal disorders that encite the dog to bite and/or scratch at the affected area. The incessant biting and scratching further irritates the skin, causing the superficial infection to become a moist weeping wound. Hot spots usually occur on the dog's hindquarters.

AUTO-IMMUNE SKIN CONDITIONS

Auto-immune skin conditions are commonly described as being allergic to yourself. Allergies, though, usually result in inflammatory reactions to an outside stimulus. Auto-immune diseases cause serious damage to the tissues which are involved.

The best known auto-immune disease is lupus. It affects people as well as dogs. The symptoms are very variable and may affect the kidneys, bones, blood chemistry

A hot spot that is constantly licked may develop into a raw open wound. Veterinary surgeons have failed to determine the cause of this problem.

and skin. It can be fatal to both dogs and humans, though it is not thought to be transmissible. It is usually successfully treated with cortisone, prednisone or similar corticosteroid, but extensive use of these drugs can have harmful side effects.

HEREDITARY SKIN DISORDERS

Veterinary dermatologists are currently researching a number of skin disorders that are believed to have an hereditary basis. These inherited diseases are transmitted by both parents, who appear (phenotypically) normal but have a recessive gene for the disease, meaning that they carry, but are not affected by, the disease. These diseases pose serious problems to breeders because in some instances there are no methods of identifying

Disease	What is it?	What causes it?	Symptoms
Leptospirosis	Severe disease that affects the internal organs; can be spread to people.	A bacterium, which is often carried by rodents, that enters through mucous membranes and spreads quickly through-out the body.	Range from fever, vomiting and loss of appetite in less severe cases to shock, irreversible kidney damage and possibly death in most severe cases.
Rabies	Potentially deadly virus that infects warm-blooded mammals. Not seen in United Kingdom.	Bite from a carrier of the virus, mainly wild animals.	1st stage: dog exhibits change in behaviour, fear. 2nd stage: dog's behaviour becomes more aggressive. 3rd stage: loss of coordination, trouble with bodily functions.
Parvovirus	Highly contagious virus, potentially deadly.	Ingestion of the virus, which is usually spread through the faeces of infected dogs.	Most common: severe diarrhoea. Also vomiting, fatigue, lack of appetite.
Kennel cough	Contagious respiratory infection.	Combination of types of bacteria and virus. Most common: *Bordetella bronchiseptica* bacteria and parainfluenza virus.	Chronic cough.
Distemper	Disease primarily affecting respiratory and nervous system.	Virus that is related to the human measles virus.	Mild symptoms such as fever, lack of appetite and mucous secretion progress to evidence of brain damage, 'hard pad.'
Hepatitis	Virus primarily affecting the liver.	Canine adenovirus type I (CAV-1). Enters system when dog breathes in particles.	Lesser symptoms include listlessness, diarrhoea, vomiting. More severe symptoms include 'blue-eye' (clumps of virus in eye).
Coronavirus	Virus resulting in digestive problems.	Virus is spread through infected dog's faeces.	Stomach upset evidenced by lack of appetite, vomiting, diarrhoea.

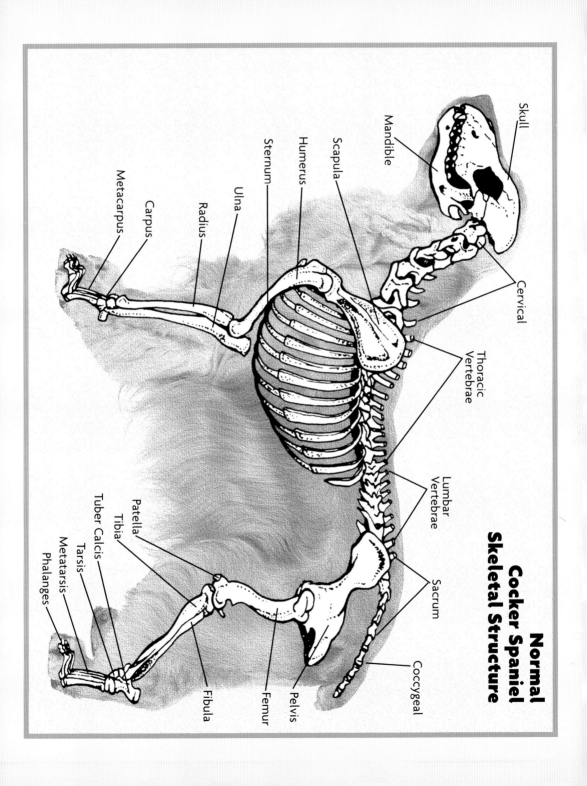

Normal
Cocker Spaniel
Skeletal Structure

carriers. Often the secondary diseases associated with these skin conditions are even more debilitating than the skin disorders themselves, including cancers and respiratory problems; others can be lethal.

FLEA REMEDIES
• Add a small amount of pennyroyal or eucalyptus oil to your dog's bath. These natural remedies repel fleas.
• Supplement your dog's food with fresh garlic (minced or grated) and a hearty amount of brewer's yeast, both of which ward off fleas.
• Use a flea comb on your dog daily. Submerge fleas in a cup of bleach to kill them quickly.
• Confine the dog to only a few rooms to limit the spread of fleas in the home.
• Vacuum daily...and get all of the crevices! Dispose of the bag every few days until the problem in under control.
• Wash your dog's bedding daily. Cover cushions where your dog sleeps with towels, and wash the towels often.

Among the hereditary skin disorders, for which the mode of inheritance is known, are acrodermatitis, cutaneous asthenia (Ehlers-Danlos syndrome), sebaceous adenitis, cyclic hematopoiesis, dermatomyositis, IgA deficiency, colour dilution alopaecia and nodular dermatofibrosis. Some of these disorders are

limited to one or two breeds, while others affect a large number of breeds. All inherited diseases must be diagnosed and treated by a veterinary specialist.

AIRBORNE ALLERGIES
Another interesting allergy is pollen allergy. Humans have hay fever, rose fever and other fevers from which they suffer during the pollinating season. Many dogs suffer the same allergies. So when the pollen count is high, your dog might suffer. Don't expect them to sneeze and have runny noses like humans. Dogs react to pollen allergies the same way they react to fleas—they scratch and bite themselves. Cocker Spaniels are very susceptible to airborne pollen allergies.

FOOD PROBLEMS
FOOD ALLERGIES
Dogs are allergic to many foods which are best-sellers and highly recommended by veterinary surgeons. Changing the brand of food that you buy may not eliminate the problem because the element of the food to which the dog is allergic may also be contained in the new brand.

Recognising a food allergy is difficult. Humans vomit or have rashes when they eat a food to which they are allergic. Dogs neither vomit nor (usually) develop a rash. Instead they itch, scratch and bite, thus making the diagnosis extremely difficult. While parasite bites are usually seasonal, food allergies are year-round problems.

FOOD INTOLERANCE
Food intolerance is the inability of the dog to completely digest certain foods. Puppies which may have done very well on their mother's milk may not do well on cow's milk. The result of this food intolerance may be loose bowels, passing gas and stomach pains. These are the only obvious symptoms to food intolerance and that makes diasgnosis difficult.

TREATING FOOD PROBLEMS
Handling food allergies and food intolerance yourself is possible. Put your dog on a diet that he has never had before. Obviously if he has never eaten this new food, he cannot have been allergic to or intolerant of it. Start with a single ingredient which is NOT in the dog's diet at the present time, such as raw tripe and wholemeal bread. Keep the dog on this diet (with no additives) for a month. If the symptoms of food allergy or intolerance disappear, do not go back to his old diet but stick to the tripe and bread and add one ingredient of his former diet. Let the dog stay on the modified diet for a month before you add another ingredient. It will take some time, but you will find out which is the ingredient that caused the problems.

> **DID YOU KNOW?**
> Never mix flea control products without first consulting your veterinary surgeon. Some products can become toxic when combined with others (a flea collar after a flea dip, etc.) and can cause serious or fatal consequences.

An alternative method is to carefully study the ingredients in the diet to which your dog is allergic or intolerable. Identify the main ingredient in this diet and eliminate the main ingredient by buying a different food which does not have that ingredient. Keep experimenting until the symptoms disappear after one month on the new diet.

EXTERNAL PARASITES
Of all the problems to which dogs are prone, none is more well known and frustrating than fleas. Fleas, which usually refers to fleas, ticks and mites, are relatively simple to cure but difficult to prevent. The opposite is true for the parasites which are harboured inside the body. They are a bit more difficult to cure but they are easier to control.

FLEAS
It is possible to control flea infestation but you have to understand the life cycle of a typical flea in order to control them. Basically fleas are a summertime problem

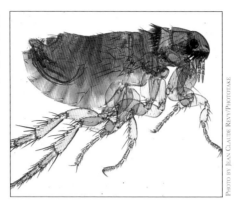

The magnified image of a male dog flea, *Ctenocephalides canis*.

PHOTO BY JEAN CLAUDE REVY/PHOTOTAKE

and their effective treatment (destruction) is environmental. The problem is that there is no single flea control medicine (insecticide) which can be used in every flea-infested area. To understand flea control you must apply suitable treatment to the weak link in the life cycle of the flea.

THE LIFE CYCLE OF A FLEA

Fleas are found in four forms: eggs, larvae, pupae and adults. You really need a low-power microscope or hand lens to identify a living flea's eggs, pupae or larva. They spend their whole

Dog flea eggs magnified.

Male cat flea, *Ctenocephalides felis*, commonly found on dogs as well as cats.

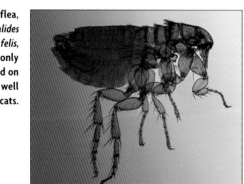

PHOTO BY JEAN CLAUDE REVY/PHOTOTAKE

DID YOU KNOW?

Average size dogs can pass 1,360,000 roundworm eggs every day.

For example, if there were only 1 million dogs in the world, the world would be saturated with 1,300 metric tonnes of dog faeces.

These faeces would contain 15,000,000,000 roundworm eggs.

7–31% of home gardens and children's play boxes in the U. S. contained roundworm eggs.

Flushing dog's faeces down the toilet is not a safe practice because the usual sewage treatments do not destroy roundworm eggs.

Infected puppies start shedding roundworm eggs at 3 weeks of age. They can be infected by their mother's milk.

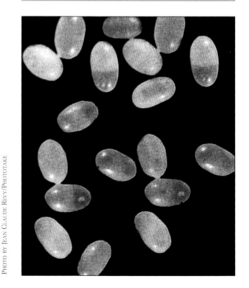

The Life Cycle of the Flea

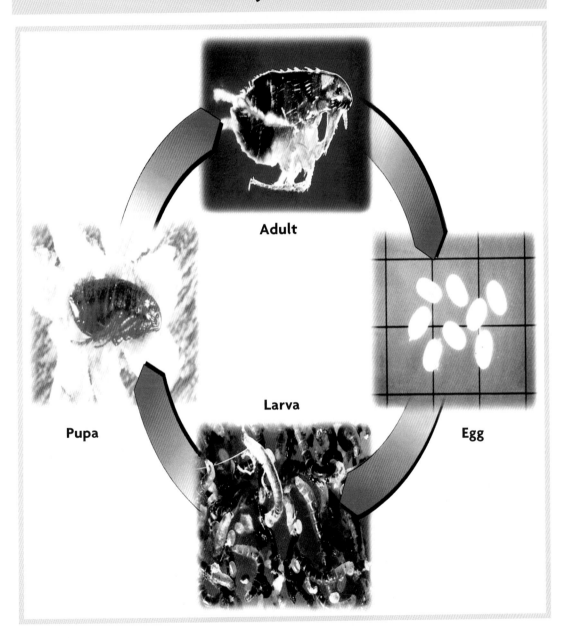

Adult

Pupa

Larva

Egg

The Life Cycle of the Flea was posterised by Fleabusters. Poster courtesy of Fleabusters®, Rx for Fleas.

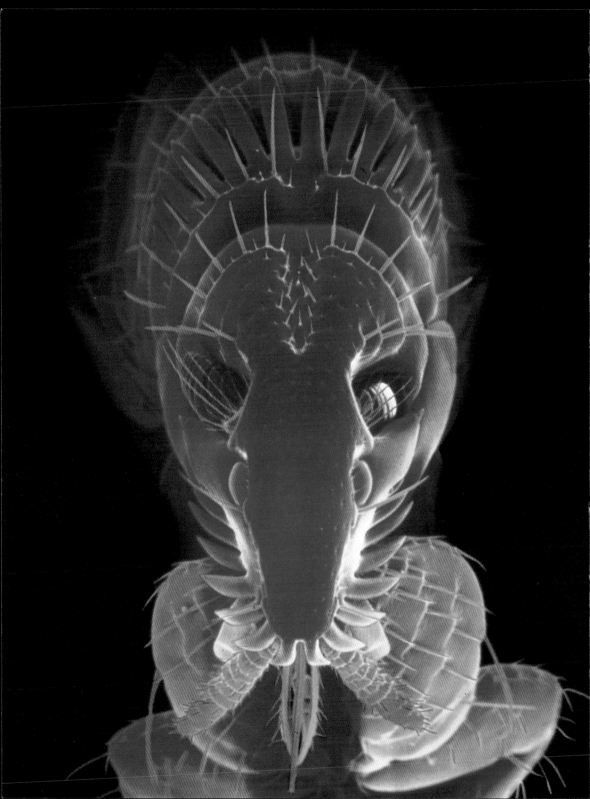

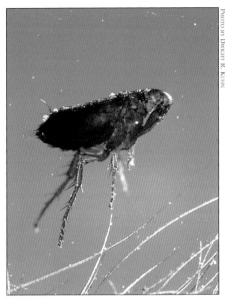

PHOTO BY DWIGHT R. KUHN

person. Yes, fleas from dogs bite people. That's why it is so important to control fleas both on the dog and in the dog's entire environment. You must, therefore, treat the dog and the environment simultaneously.

DE-FLEAING THE HOME

Cleanliness is the simple rule. If you have a cat living with your dog, the matter is more complicated since most dog fleas are actually cat fleas. But since cats climb onto many areas that are never accessible to dogs (like

An exceptional action photo showing a flea jumping from a dog's back.

FACING PAGE: A scanning electron micrograph of a dog or cat flea, *Ctenocephalides*, enlarged, magnified and coloured for effect.

lives on your Cocker unless they are forcibly removed by brushing, bathing, scratching or biting.

Several species infest both dog and cats. The dog flea is scientifically known as *Ctenocephalides canis* while the cat flea is *Ctenocephalides felis*. Cat fleas are very common on dogs.

Fleas lay eggs while they are in residence on your dog. These eggs do not adhere to the hair of your dog and they simply fall off almost as soon as they dry (they may be a bit damp when initially laid). These eggs are the reservoir of future flea infestations. If your dog scratches himself and is able to dislodge a few fleas, they simply fall off and await a future chance to attack a dog...or even a

S.E.M. BY DR. DENNIS KUNKEL, UNIVERSITY OF HAWAII.

An S.E.M. (scanning electron micrograph), magnified and computer coloured, of a dog flea, *Ctenocephalides canis*.

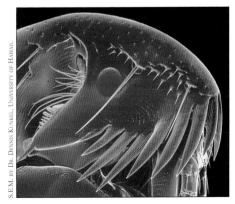

S.E.M. BY DR. DENNIS KUNKEL, UNIVERSITY OF HAWAII.

The head of the dog flea *Ctenocephalides canis*, magnified by a scanning electron microscope.

127

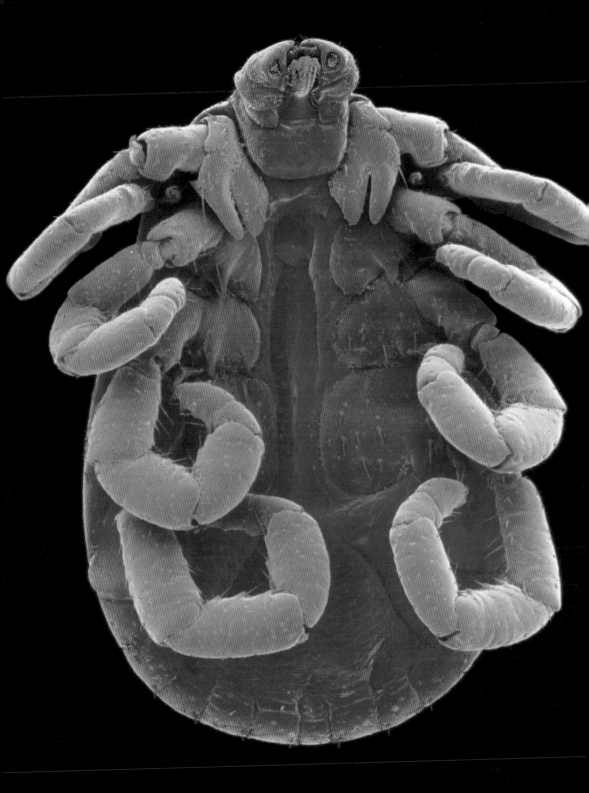

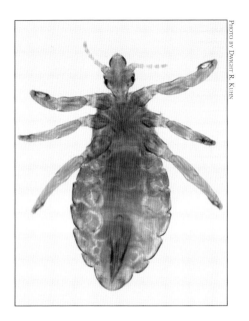

Photo by Dwight R. Kuhn

windowsills, tabletops, etc.), you have to clean all of these areas too. The hard floor surfaces (tiles, wood, stone and linoleum) must be mopped several times a day. Drops of food onto the floor are actually food for flea larvae! All rugs and furniture must be vacuumed several times a day. Don't forget cupboards, under furniture and cushions. A study has reported that a vacuum cleaner with a beater bar can only remove 20% of the larvae and 50% of the eggs. The vacuum bags should be discarded into a sealed plastic bag or burned. The vacuum machine itself should be cleaned. The outdoor area to which your dog has access must also be treated with an insecticide.

Human lice look like dog lice; the two are very closely related.

FACING PAGE: The dog tick, *Dermacentor variabilis*, is the most common tick found on Cocker Spaniels. Look at the eight legs! No wonder ticks are difficult to remove.

DID YOU KNOW?
There are many parasiticides which can be used around your home and garden to control fleas.

Natural pyrethrins can be used inside the house.

Allethrin, bioallethrin, permethrin and resmethrin can also be used inside the house but permethrin has been used successfully outdoors, too.

Carbaryl can be used indoors and outdoors.

Propoxur can be used indoors.

Chlorpyrifos, diazinon and malathion can be used indoors or outdoors and it has an extended residual activity.

Ticks can only live by ingesting blood.

Your vet will be able to recommend a household insecticidal spray, but this must be used with caution and instructions strictly adhered to.

While there are many drugs available to kill fleas on the dog itself, such as the miracle drug ivermectin, it is best to have the de-fleaing and de-worming supervised by your vet.

129

DID YOU KNOW?

There are drugs which prevent fleas from maturing from egg to adult.

The weak link is the maturation from a larva to a pupa.

Methoprene and fenoxycarb mimic the effect of maturation enhancers, thus, in effect, killing the larva before it pupates.

Methoprene is mildly effective in killing flea eggs while fenoxycarb is better able to stand UV rays from the sun. There is a combination of both drugs which has an effective life of 6 months and destroys 93% of the flea population.

There are desiccants which dry out the eggs, larvae and adult fleas. These desiccants are common, well known and do not usually affect dogs, cats, humans or other mammalian animals.

Desiccants include silica gel, sodium borate and diatomaceous earth. The best known and most effective is polymerized borate which is marketed by Rx for Fleas Plus® (Fleabusters®).

Ivermectin is effective against many external and internal parasites including heartworms, roundworms, tapeworms, flukes, ticks and mites. It has not been approved for use to control these pests, but veterinary surgeons frequently use it anyway.

STERILISING THE ENVIRONMENT

Besides cleaning your home with vacuum cleaners and mops, you have to treat the outdoor range of your dog. This means trimming bushes, spreading insecticide and being careful not to poison areas in which fishes or other animals reside.

This is best done by an outside service specialising in defleaing. Your vet should be able to recommend a local service.

TICKS AND MITES

Though not as common as fleas, ticks and mites are found all over the tropical and temperate world. They do not bite like fleas; rather, they harpoon. They dig their sharp proboscis (nose) into the dog's skin and drink the blood. Their only food and drink is dog's blood. Dogs can get Lyme disease, Rocky Mountain spotted fever (normally found in the U.S.A. only), paralysis and many other maladies from ticks and mites. They may live where fleas are found except they like to hide in cracks or seams in walls wherever dogs live. They are controlled the same way fleas are controlled.

The dog tick *Dermacentor variabilis* may well be the most common dog tick in many geographical areas, especially those areas where the climate is hot and humid.

Most dog ticks have life expectancies of a week to six months, depending upon climatic conditions. They can neither jump nor fly, but they can crawl slowly and can range up to 5 metres (16 feet) to reach a sleeping or unsuspecting dog.

MANGE

Mites cause a skin irritation called mange. Some are contagious, like *Cheyletiella*, ear mites, scabies and chiggers. The non-contagious mites are *Demodex*. The most serious of the mites is the ear mite infestation. Ear mites are usually controlled with ivermectin.

It is essential that your dog be treated for mange as quickly as possible because some forms of mange are transmissible to people.

S.E.M. BY DR. DENNIS KUNKEL, UNIVERSITY OF HAWAII.

The head of the dog tick, *Dermacentor variabilis*, magnified and colourised.

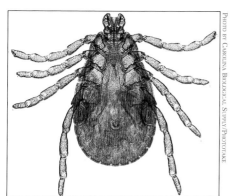

PHOTO BY CAROLINA BIOLOGICAL SUPPLY/PHOTOTAKE

their hosts (symbiosis), while the dumb parasites kill their host. Most of the worm infections are relatively easy to control. If they are not controlled, they eventually weaken the host dog to the point that other medical problems occur, but they are not dumb parasites.

A brown dog tick, *Rhipicephalus sanguineus.*

INTERNAL PARASITES

Most animals—fishes, birds and mammals, including dogs and humans—have worms and other parasites which live inside their bodies. According to Dr. Herbert R. Axelrod, the fish pathologist, there are two kinds of parasites: dumb and smart. The smart parasites live in peaceful co-operation with

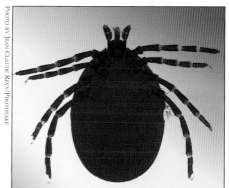

PHOTO BY JEAN CLAUDE REVY/PHOTOTAKE

An uncommon dog tick of the genus *Ixode*, magnified and colourised.

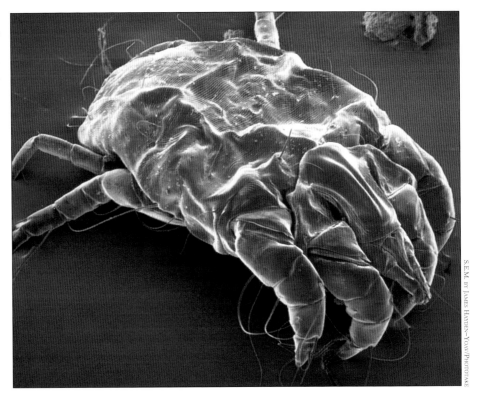

The mange mite, *Psoroptes bovis*, magnified more than 200 times.

S.E.M. BY JAMES HAYDEN–YOAV/PHOTOTAKE

ROUNDWORMS

The roundworms that infect dogs are scientifically known as *Toxocara canis.* They live in the dog's intestines. The worms shed eggs continually. It has been estimated that a dog produces about 100 grams of faeces every day. Each gram of faeces averages 10,000-12,000 eggs of roundworms. There are no known areas in which dogs roam that do not contain the eggs of roundworms. The greatest danger of roundworms is that they infect people, too! It is wise to have your dog tested regularly for roundworms.

Pigs also have roundworm infections, which can be passed to humans and dogs. The typical pig roundworm parasite is called *Ascaris lumbricoides.*

HOOKWORMS

The worm *Ancylostoma caninum* is commonly called the dog hookworm. It is dangerous to humans and cats. It also has teeth by which it attaches itself to the intestines of the dog. Because it changes the site of its attachment about six times a day, the dog loses blood from each detachment, possibly causing iron-deficiency anaemia. They are easily purged from the dog with many medications, the best of which seems to be ivermectin. Hookworms rarely infect dogs in Britain unless they have access to grasslands.

TAPEWORMS

There are many species of tapeworms. They are carried by fleas! The dog eats the flea and thus starts the tapeworm cycle. Humans can also be infected with tapeworms, so don't eat fleas! Fleas are so small that your dog could pass them onto your hands, your plate or your food and thus make it possible for you to ingest a flea which is carrying tapeworm eggs.

While tapeworm infection is not life threatening in dogs (smart parasite!), it can be the cause of a very serious liver

The roundworm, *Ascaris lumbricoides.*

The roundworm, *Rhabditis.*

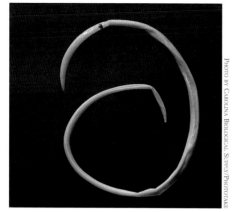

PHOTO BY CAROLINA BIOLOGICAL SUPPLY/PHOTOTAKE

Male and female hookworms, *Ancylostoma caninum,* are rarely seen in Britain.

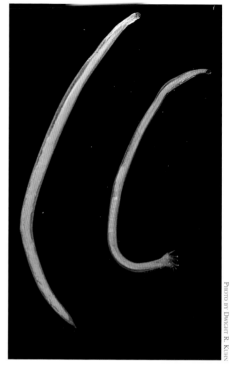

PHOTO BY DWIGHT R. KUHN

DID YOU KNOW?

Humans, rats, squirrels, foxes, wolves, mixed breeds of dogs and purebred dogs are all susceptible to tapeworm infection. Except for humans, tapeworms are usually not a fatal infection.

Infected individuals can harbour a thousand parasitic worms.

If dogs eat infected rats or mice, they get the tapeworm disease.

One month after attaching to a dog's intestine, the worm starts shedding eggs. These eggs are infective immediately.

Infective eggs can live for a few months without a host animal.

Roundworms, hookworms, whipworms and tapeworms are just a few of the commonly known worms which infect dogs.

disease for humans. About 50 percent of the humans infected with *Echinococcus multilocularis,* causing alveolar hydatis, perish.

HEARTWORMS

Heartworms are thin, extended worms up to 30 cm (12 in.) long which live in a dog's heart and major blood vessels around the heart. Cocker Spaniels may have up to 200 of these worms. The symptoms may be loss of energy, loss of appetite, coughing, the development of a pot belly and anaemia.

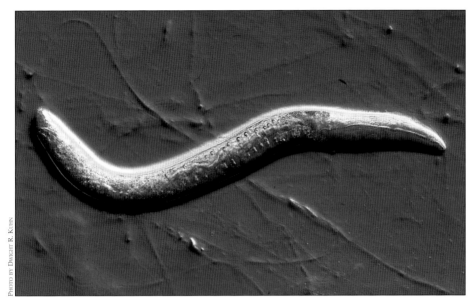

PHOTO BY DWIGHT R. KUHN

The roundworm, *Ascaris lumbricoides*, infects humans, dogs and pigs.

Heartworms are transmitted by mosquitoes. The mosquito drinks the blood of an infected dog and takes in larvae with the blood. The larvae, called microfilaria, develop within the body of the mosquito and are passed on to the next dog bitten after the larvae mature. It takes 2–3 weeks for the larvae to develop to the infective stage within the body of the mosquito. Dogs should be treated at about 6 weeks of age, then every 6 months.

Blood testing for heartworms is not necessarily indicative of how seriously your dog is infected. This is a dangerous disease. Heartworm is becoming more common in the United Kingdom.

DID YOU KNOW?

Ridding your puppy of worms is VERY IMPORTANT because certain worms that puppies carry can infect humans, such as tapeworms, hookworms and roundworms.

Since puppies are never housebroken at two to three weeks of age, it is easy for them to pass on the parasites (worms) to humans.

Breeders initiate a deworming programme two weeks after weaning. The routine is repeated every two or three weeks until the puppy is three months old. The breeder from whom you obtained your puppy should provide you with the complete details of the deworming programme. Your veterinary surgeon can prescribe and monitor the programme.

DID YOU KNOW?
Flea-killers are poisonous. You should not spray these toxic chemicals on areas of the dog's body that he licks, on his genitals or on his face. Flea-killers taken internally are a better answer, but check with your vet in case internal therapy is not advised for your dog.

BREED-RELATED HEREDITARY CONDITIONS
FAMILIAL NEPHROPATHY (FN)
This is a very serious kidney disease in young Cocker Spaniels which has been present in the breed for at least 30 years. Signs of the disease are first seen from 12 weeks to 2½ years of age. Once kidney failure begins, most pups fail to put on weight, then lose weight, start to become sick and eat less. Some show an increase in thirst and in urine output. A few develop diarrhoea. Most pups then have less than two months before they become so ill that they have to be put down. There is no treatment available and the outcome is inevitable. FN is inherited as a simple recessive, which means that both parents should carry the gene to produce affected progeny.

HIP DYSPLASIA
This is a genetic problem whereby the acetabulum (hip socket), into which the femoral head (knuckle bone) rests, degenerates. It can only be diagnosed by scrutiny of an x-ray plate, which is done by specialists trained to do so. The B.V.A. (British Veterinary Association) manages a joint scheme with The Kennel Club, and on the Continent the universities in the various countries have established, together with the F.C.I. (Fédération Cynologique Internationale), international classifications.

It is not a problem that affects Cocker Spaniels very much, although the occurrence is slightly higher in solid-coloured than in parti-coloured Cockers. That does not mean that breeders should not be careful. Most breeders x-ray all of the dogs they use for breeding and eliminate those dogs with a high hip score (denoting dysplasia) from their breeding programmes.

DID YOU KNOW?
Not every dog's ears are the same. Ears that are open to the air are healthier than ears with poor air circulation. Sometimes a dog can have two differently shaped ears. You should not probe inside your dog's ears. Only clean that which is accessible with a wad of soft cotton wool.

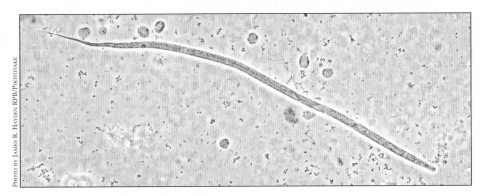

The heartworm, *Dirofilaria immitis.*

PHOTO BY JAMES R. HAYDEN RPB/PHOTOTAKE

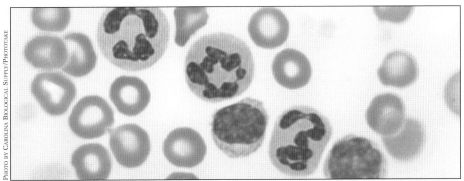

Magnified heartworm larvae, *Dirofilaria immitis.*

PHOTO BY CAROLINA BIOLOGICAL SUPPLY/PHOTOTAKE

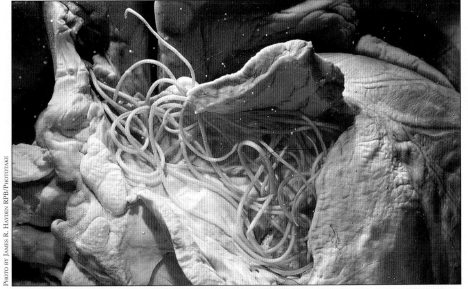

This surgically opened dog's heart is infected with canine heartworm, *Dirofilaria immitis.*

PHOTO BY JAMES R. HAYDEN RPB/PHOTOTAKE

137

Progressive Retinal Atrophy (PRA)

PRA is a congenital disease of the eye that is causing much concern in canine circles. It is hereditary and it is inherited through a recessive gene, i.e. that both parents must be carrier of the gene to produce afflicted offspring. The symptoms rarely manifest themselves until a dog is mature, sometimes even 6 or 7 years of age, so that the dog or bitch may well have been used for breeding. The disease can only be diagnosed by a specialist with special equipment. In many countries eye testing is obligatory if one wants to breed and the results of the eye tests are published. PRA is mostly seen in parti-coloured Cocker Spaniels.

Cataracts

A cataract is a condition whereby the lens of the eyes will become covered with a milky film and the dog's eyesight will be seriously affected. It is often found in older dogs. However, cataracts can also be inherited and affect young Cockers. Dogs that are being tested for PRA will normally also be tested for the presence of cataracts. Contrary to PRA, cataracts can occur in one eye only.

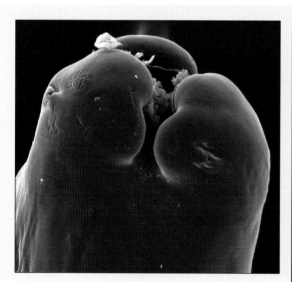

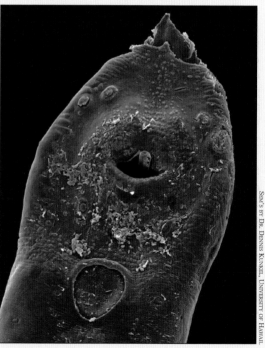

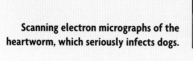

Scanning electron micrographs of the heartworm, which seriously infects dogs.

138

SEM'S BY DR. DENNIS KUNKEL, UNIVERSITY OF HAWAII.

When Your Cocker Spaniel Gets Old

The term old is a qualitative term. For dogs, as well as their masters, old is relative. Certainly we can all distinguish between a puppy and an adult Cocker Spaniel—there are the obvious physical traits, such as size and appearance, and personality traits, like their antics and the expressions on their faces. Puppies that are nasty are very rare. Puppies and young dogs like to play with children. Children's natural exuberance is a good match for the seemingly endless energy of young dogs. They like to run, jump, chase and retrieve. When dogs grow up and cease their interaction with children, they are often thought of as being too old to play with the kids.

On the other hand, if a Cocker Spaniel is only exposed to people over 60 years of age, its life will normally be less active and it will not seem to be getting old as soon as its activity level slows down.

If people live to be 100 years old, dogs live to be 20 years old. While this is a good rule of thumb, it is VERY inaccurate. When trying to compare dog years to human years, you cannot make a generalisation about all dogs. You can make the generalisation that, say, 13 years is a good life span for a Cocker, but you cannot compare it to that of a Chihuahua or a Great Dane, as many small breeds typically live longer than large breeds. Dogs are generally considered mature within three years. They can reproduce even earlier. So the first three years of a dog's life are more like seven

When your Cocker gets old, he'll slow down and become less active. You should recognise these signs and alter your routine accordingly.

139

DID YOU KNOW?

An old dog starts to show one or more of the following symptoms:

• The hair on its face and paws starts to turn grey. The colour breakdown usually starts around the eyes and mouth.

• The exercise routine becomes more and more tedious and the dog almost refuses to join exercises that it previously enjoyed.

• Food intake diminishes.

• Responses to calls, whistles and other signals are ignored more and more.

• Eye contacts indicate aloofness and do not evoke tail wagging (assuming they always did).

times that of comparable humans. That means a three-year-old dog is like a 21-year-old person. As the curve of comparison shows, there is no hard and fast rule for comparing dog and human ages. The comparison is made even more difficult, for not all humans age at the same rate...and human females live longer than human males.

WHAT TO DO WHEN THE TIME COMES

You are never fully prepared to make a rational decision about putting your dog to sleep. It is very obvious that you love your Cocker or you would not be reading this book. Putting a loved dog to sleep is extremely difficult. It is

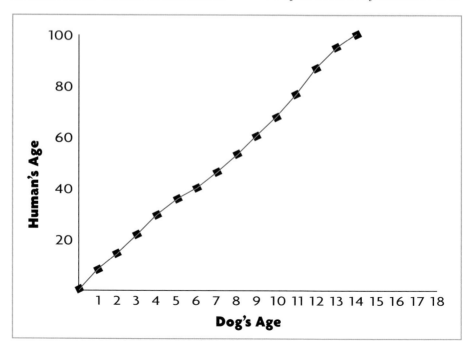

a decision that must be made with your veterinary surgeon. You are usually forced to make the decision when one of the life-threatening symptoms listed above becomes serious enough for you to seek medical (veterinary) help.

If the prognosis of the malady indicates the end is near and your beloved pet will only suffer more and experience no enjoyment for the balance of its life, then there is no choice but euthanasia.

Senior Cocker Spaniels display a certain dignity that commands respect. This is Styvechale Storm Cloud at age 14 years.

DID YOU KNOW?

The symptoms listed below are symptoms that gradually appear and gradually become more noticeable. They are not life threatening, however, the symptoms below are to be taken very seriously and a discussion with your veterinary surgeon is warranted:

• Your dog cries and whimpers when it moves and stops running completely.

• Convulsions start or become more serious and frequent. The usual convulsion (spasm) is when the dog stiffens and starts to tremble being unable or unwilling to move. The seizure usually lasts for 5 to 30 minutes.

• More and more toilet accidents occur. Urine and bowel movements take place indoors without warning.

• Vomiting becomes more and more frequent.

WHAT IS EUTHANASIA?

Euthanasia derives from the Greek meaning good death. In other words, it means the planned, painless killing of a dog suffering from a painful, incurable condition, or who is so aged that it cannot walk, see, eat or control its excretory functions.

Euthanasia is usually accomplished by injection with an overdose of an anaesthesia or barbiturate. Aside from the prick of the needle, the experience is painless.

HOW ABOUT YOU?

The days during which the dog becomes ill and the end occurs can be unusually stressful for you. If this is your first experience with the death of a loved one, you may need the comfort dictated by your religious beliefs. If you are the

DID YOU KNOW?
The bottom line is simply that a dog is getting old when YOU think it is getting old because it slows down in its general activities, including walking, running, eating, jumping and retrieving. On the other hand, certain activities increase, like more sleeping, more licking your hands and body, more barking and more repetition of habits like going to the door when you put your coat on without being called.

HOW ABOUT THE FINAL RESTING PLACE?

Dogs can have the same privileges as humans. They can be buried in their entirety in a pet cemetery (very expensive) in a burial container, buried in your garden in a place suitably marked with a stone or newly planted tree or bush, cremated with the ashes being given to you, or even stuffed and mounted by a taxidermist.

All of these options should be discussed frankly and openly with your veterinary surgeon. Do not be afraid to ask financial questions. Cremations are usually mass burning and the ashes you

head of the family and have children, you should have involved them in the decision of putting your Cocker to sleep. In any case, euthanasia alone is painful and stressful for the family of the dog. But just as hard is the decision-making process.

Usually your dog can be maintained on drugs for a few days while it is kept in the clinic in order to give you ample time to make a decision. During this time, talking with members of the family or religious representatives, or even people who have lived through this same experience, can ease the burden of your inevitable decision...but then what?

Some pet cemeteries have inexpensive sites in which you can store your deceased ashes.

get may not be the ashes of your beloved dog. If you want a private cremation, this can usually be arranged. However, this may be a little more expensive.

GETTING ANOTHER DOG?

The grief of losing your beloved dog will be as lasting as the grief of losing a human friend or rela-

DID YOU KNOW?
The more open discussion you have about the whole stressful occurrence, the easier it will be for you when the time comes.

When Your Cocker Spaniel Gets Old

Signs the Owner Can Look For

IF YOU NOTICE...	IT COULD INDICATE...
Discolouration of teeth and gums, foul breath, loss of appetite	Abcesses, gum disease, mouth lesions
Lumps, bumps, cysts, warts, fatty tumours	Cancers, benign or malignant
Cloudiness of eyes, apparent loss of sight.	Cataracts, lenticular sclerosis, PRA, retinal dysplasia, blindness
Flaky coat, alopaecia (hair loss)	Hormonal problems, hypothyroidism
Obesity, appetite loss, excessive weight gain	Various problems
Household accidents, increased urination	Diabetes, kidney or bladder disease
Increased thirst	Kidney disease, diabetes mellitus
Change in sleeping habits, coughing	Heart disease
Difficulty moving	Arthritis, degenerative joint disease, spondylosis (degenerative spine disease)

**If the owner notices any of these signs,
an appointment should be made immediately
with the veterinary surgeon for a thorough evaluation.**

DID YOU KNOW?

Your senior dog may lose interest in eating, not because he's less hungry but because his senses of smell and taste have diminished. The old chow simply does not smell as good as it once did. Additionally, older dogs use less energy and thereby can sustain themselves on less food.

Cemeteries for pets exist. Consult your veterinary surgeon to help you locate one.

tive. You cannot go out and buy another grandfather, but you can go out and buy another Cocker Spaniel. In most cases, if your dog died of old age (if there is such a thing), it had slowed down considerably. Do you want a new Cocker puppy to replace it? Or are you better off in finding a more mature Cocker, say two to three years of age, which will usually be housebroken and will have an already developed personality. In

DID YOU KNOW?

Euthanasia must be done by a licensed veterinary surgeon. There also may be societies for the prevention of cruelty to animals in your area. They often offer this service upon a vet's recommendation.

this case, you can find out if you like each other after a few hours of being together.

The decision is, of course, your own. Do you want another Cocker? Perhaps you want a smaller or larger dog? How much do you want to spend on a dog? Consult your local shelter or rescue organisation to adopt a dog. Ask the breed club whether there are any rescue dogs looking for a new home.

Whatever you decide, do it as quickly as possible. Most people usually buy the same breed they had before because they know (and love) the characteristics of that breed. Then, too, they often know people who have the same breed and perhaps they are lucky enough that one of their friends expects a litter soon. What could be better?

Showing Your Cocker Spaniel

Is the puppy you selected growing into a handsome representative of his breed? You are rightly proud of your handsome little tyke, and he has mastered nearly all of the basic obedience commands that you have taught him. How about attending a dog show and seeing how the other half of the dog-loving world lives! Even if you never imagined yourself standing in the centre ring at Crufts Dog Show, why not dream a little?

WINNING THE TICKET

Earning a championship at Kennel Club shows is the most difficult in the world. Compared to the United States and Canada where it is relatively not 'challenging,' collecting three green tickets not only requires much time and effort, it can be very expensive! Challenge Certificates, as the tickets are properly known, are the building blocks of champions—good breeding, good handling, good training and good luck!

UNDERSTANDING DOG SHOWS

The first concept that the canine neophyte learns when watching a dog show is that each breed first competes against members of its own breed. Once the judge has selected the best member of each breed, then that chosen dog will compete with other dogs of his classification. Finally, the best of each group will compete for Best of Show and Reserve Best in Show.

The second concept that you must understand is that the dogs are not actually competing with

Speaking of the centre ring at Crufts, here's the Supreme Champion of the 1996 show, Sh. Ch. Caniou Cambrai, owned by Patricia Bentley.

145

Learning to stand your Cocker to display his best attributes is half of the battle of showing. Clever handling, however, can only fool the less-clever judge.

It just doesn't get any better than Best in Show at Crufts. Following the tradition of Exquisite Model of Ware and Tracy Witch of Ware, here's Sh. Ch. Caniou Cambrai reigning as Supreme Champion.

one another. The judge compares each dog against the breed standard, which is a written description of the ideal specimen of the breed. This imaginary dog never walked into a show ring, has never been bred and, to the woe of dog breeders around the globe, does not exist. Breeders

attempt to get as close to this ideal as possible, with every litter, but theoretically the 'perfect' dog is so elusive that it is impossible. (And if the 'perfect' dog were born, breeders and judges would never agree that it was indeed 'perfect.')

If you are interested in exploring dog shows, your best bet is to join your local breed club. These clubs host shows (often matches and open shows for beginners), send out newsletters, offer training days and provide an outlet to meet members who are often friendly and generous with their advice and contacts. To locate the nearest breed club for you, contact The Kennel Club, the ruling body for the British dog world, not just for conformation shows, but for working trials, obedience trials, agility trials and field trials. The Kennel Club furnishes the rules and regulations for all these events plus general dog registration and other

DID YOU KNOW?

Just like with anything else, there is a certain etiquette to the show ring that can only be learned through experience. Showing your dog can be quite intimidating to you as a novice when it seems as if everyone else knows what he's doing. You can familiarise yourself with ring procedure beforehand by taking a class to prepare you and your dog for conformation showing or by talking with an experienced handler. When you are in the ring, listen and pay attention to the judge and follow his/her directions. Remember, even the most skilled handlers had to start somewhere. Keep it up and you too will be a pro in no time!

basic requirements of dog ownership. Its annual show, held in Birmingham, is the largest bench show in England. Every year no fewer than 20,000 of the U.K.'s best dogs qualify to participate in a marvellous show lasting four days.

There are different kinds of shows. At the most competitive and prestigious of these shows, the Championship Shows, a dog can earn Challenge Certificates, and thereby become a 'champion.' A dog must earn three Challenge Certificates under three different judges to earn the prefix of 'Sh. Ch.' or 'Ch.' Note that some breeds must qualify in a field trial

CLASSES AT DOG SHOWS

There can be as many as 18 classes per sex for your breed. Check the show schedule carefully to make sure that you have entered your dog in the appropriate class. Among the classes offered can be: Minor Puppy (ages 6 to 9 months); Puppy (ages 6 to 12 months); Junior (ages 6 to 18 months); Beginners (handler or dog never won first place); as well as the following, each of which is defined in the schedule: Maiden; Novice; Tyro; Debutant; Undergraduate; Graduate; Postgraduate; Minor Limit; Mid Limit; Limit; Open; Veteran; Stud Dog; Brood Bitch; Progeny; Brace; and Team.

A Cocker Spaniel competing at a local show in the Netherlands. There are many lovely Cockers bred on the Continent, and they are always popular at the shows.

The top Cocker Spaniel bitch and best home-bred Cocker in Holland in 1998 was the Dutch and German Champion Speggle-Waggel's Quible.

in order to gain the title of full champion. Challenge Certificates are awarded to a very small percentage of the dogs competing, and the number of Challenge Certificates awarded in any one year is based upon the total number of dogs in each breed entered for competition. There are three types of Championship Shows, a general show, where all breeds recognised by The Kennel Club can enter, a Group show, and a breed show, which is limited to only a single breed.

Sh.Ch. Quettadene Make Believe was European Champion in 1997. She lives in Hungary.

Open Shows are generally less competitive and are frequently used as 'practice shows' for young dogs. These shows, of which there are hundreds each year, can be invitingly social events and are great first show experiences for the novice. If you're just considering watching a show to wet your paws, an Open Show is a great choice.

While Championship and Open Shows are most important

for the beginner to understand, there are other types of shows in which the interested dog owner can participate. Training clubs, for example, sponsor Matches that can be entered on the day of the show for a nominal fee. These introductory level exhibitions are uniquely run: two dogs are pulled from a raffle and 'matched,' the winner of that match goes on to the next round, and eventually only one dog is left undefeated.

Exemption shows are similar in that they are simply fun classes and usually held in conjunction with small agricultural shows. Primary shows can also be

DID YOU KNOW?
The Kennel Club divides its dogs into seven Groups: Gundogs, Utility, Working, Toy, Terrier, Hounds and Pastoral.*

The Pastoral Group, established in 1999, includes those sheepdog breeds previously categorised in the Working Group.

entered on the day of the event and dogs entered must not have won anything towards their titles. Sanction and Limited shows must be entered well in advance, and there are limitations upon who can enter. Regardless of which type show you choose to begin with, you and your dog will have a grand time competing and learning your way about the shows.

Before you actually step into the ring, you would be well advised to sit back and observe the judge's ring procedure. If it is your first time in the ring, do not

---

HOW TO ENTER A DOG SHOW

1. Obtain an entry form and show schedule from the Show Secretary.
2. Select the classes that you want to enter and complete the entry form.
3. Transfer your dog into your name at The Kennel Club. (Be sure that this matter is handled before entering.)
4. Find out how far in advance show entries must be made. Oftentimes it's more than a couple of months.

---

be over-anxious and run to the front of the line. It is much better when you can stand back and study how the exhibitor in front of you is performing. The judge asks each handler to 'stand' the dog, hopefully showing the dog off to his best advantage. The judge will observe the dog from a distance and from different angles, approach the dog, check his teeth, overall structure, alertness and musculature, as well as consider how well the dog

'conforms' to the standard. Most importantly, the judge will have the exhibitor move the dog around the ring in some pattern that he or she should specify (another advantage to not going first, but always listen since some judges change their directions, and the judge is always right!) Finally the judge will give the dog one last look before moving on to the next exhibitor.

If you are not in the top three at your first show, do not be discouraged. Be patient and

Show Champion Cilleine Echelon was the top Cocker in Britain in 1981, 1982 and 1983. He was also the sire of eight British Show Champions and probably many more abroad.

The judge thoroughly examines the Cocker Spaniel on the table. The handler's job is to keep the dog calm but alert as it accepts the judge's examination.

This is an historic photo showing the winner of the 1996 Crufts Best in Show *immediately* after it was announced.

consistent and you will eventually find yourself in the winning lineup. Remember that the winners were once in your shoes and have devoted many hours and much money to earn the placement. If you find that your dog is losing every time and never getting a nod, it may be time to consider a different dog sport or just to enjoy your Cocker Spaniel as a pet.

AGILITY TRIALS

Agility began in the United Kingdom in 1977 and has since spread around the world, especially to the United States, where it enjoys strong popularity.

One of the most important of the modern sires is Sh.Ch. Scolys Starduster.

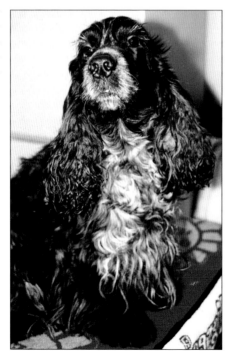

The handler directs his dog over an obstacle course that includes jumps (such as those used in the working trials), as well as tyres, the dog walk, weave poles, pipe tunnels, collapsed tunnels, etc. The Kennel Club requires that dogs not be trained for agility until they are 15 months old. This dog sport intends to be great fun for dog and owner, and interested owners should join a training club that has obstacles and experienced agility handlers who can introduce you and your dog to the 'ropes' (and tyres, tunnels and so on).

WORKING TRIALS

Working trials can be entered by any well-trained dog of any breed, not just Gundogs or Working dogs. Many dogs that earn the Kennel Club Good Citizen Dog award choose to participate in a working trial. There are three stakes at both open and championship levels: Companion Dog (CD), Utility Dog (UD) and Working Dog (WD). Like in conformation shows, dogs compete against a standard and if the dog reaches the qualifying mark, it obtains a certificate. Divided into groups, each exercise must be achieved 70 percent in order to qualify. If the dog achieves 80 percent in the open level, it receives a Certificate of Merit (COM); in the championship level, it receives a Qualifying Certificate. At the CD stake, dogs must participate in four groups, Control, Stays, Agility and Retrieving and Nosework. At the next three levels, UD, WD and TD, there are only three groups: Control, Agility and Nosework.

Agility consists of three jumps: a vertical scale, a six-foot wall of planks; a clear jump, a basic three-foot hurdle with a removable top bar; and a long jump of angled planks stretching nine feet.

To earn the UD and WD dogs must track approximately one-half mile for articles laid from one-half hour to three hours ago. Fresh ground is used for each participant.

This puppy looked very promising when it was seven weeks old...

At seven months of age it is filling out and looking even better...

At two years of age it became a full-fledged champion having won championships in Holland, Germany and Monaco in 1989...

The dog is known as Ch. Speggle-Waggel's Haighla.

WORKING TESTS AND FIELD TRIALS

Working tests are frequently used to prepare dogs for field trials, the purpose of which is to heighten the instincts and natural abilities of gundogs. Live game is not used in working tests. Unlike field trials, working tests do not count toward a dog's record at the Kennel Club, though the same judges often oversee working tests. Field trials began in England in 1947, and are only moderately popular among dog folk. While breeders of Working and Gundog breeds concern themselves with the field abilities of their dogs, there is considerably less interest

DID YOU KNOW?

You can get information about dog shows from kennel clubs and breed clubs:

Fédération Cynologique Internationale
14, rue Leopold II, B-6530 Thuin, Belgium
www.fci.be

The Kennel Club
1-5 Clarges St., Piccadilly, London W1Y 8AB, UK
www.thekennelclub.org.uk

American Kennel Club
5580 Centerview Dr., Raleigh, NC 27606-3390, USA
www.akc.org

Canadian Kennel Club
89 Skyway Ave., Suite 100, Etobicoke, Ontario M9W 6R4 Canada
www.ckc.ca

Top Cocker Spaniel and Top Dog All Breeds in the Netherlands in 1998 was the Dutch Ch. Cornbow Ensign.

in field trials than dog shows. In order for dogs to become full champions, certain breeds must qualify in the field as well. Upon gaining three CCs in the show ring, the dog is designated a Show Champion (Sh. Ch.). The title Champion (Ch) requires that the dog gain an award at a field trial, be a 'special qualifier' at a field trial or pass a 'special show dog qualifier' judged by a field trial judge on a shooting day.

Should your pupil really be talented you can go on from there to train him for field trials. It will take a lot of your time and patience and dedication but the rewards are well worth it.

FÉDÉRATION CYNOLOGIQUE INTERNATIONALE

Established in 1911, the Fédération Cynologique Internationale represents the 'world kennel clubs,' the international body brings uniformity to the breeding, judging and showing of purebred dogs. Although the FCI originally included only European nations, namely France, Germany, Holland, Austria and

Earning ribbons in the conformation ring brings prestige and pride to the Cocker owner. To become a full Champion, a Cocker must also qualify in the field.

A judge's first impression of a dog is the condition of its coat. A shiny coat on a well-groomed dog is inviting to a judge's eyes.

If you are training your dog to stand, practise whenever possible. Before you can show your dog in the breed ring, you should teach the dog to pose in a variety of situations.

This is any dog lover's most memorable moment in life! Your Cocker takes Best in Show!

Belgium, the latter of which remains the headquarters, the organisation today embraces nations on six continents and recognises well over 300 breeds of purebred dog. There are three titles attainable through the FCI: the International Champion, which is the most prestigious; the International Beauty Champion, which is based on aptitude certificates in different countries; and the International Trial Champion, which is based on achievement in obedience trials in different countries. Of course, quarantine laws in some countries prohibit some exhibitors from entering FCI shows, though many countries do participate in these impressive canine spectacles, the largest of which is the World Dog Show, hosted in a different country each year. International shows are held under the F.C.I. rules. At national shows the hosting country determines the judging system and the F.C.I. breed standards are always those of the breed's country of origin.

You and your Cocker may not speak the same language, but you don't have to be a mind-reader to understand your dog. Facial expression is often a very good indication of a dog's mood.

Understanding Your Dog's Behaviour

As a Cocker Spaniel owner, you have selected your dog so that you and your loved ones can have a companion, a playmate, a friend and a four-legged family member. You invest time, money and effort to care for and train the family's new charge. Of course, this chosen canine behaves perfectly! Well, perfectly like a dog.

THINK LIKE A DOG

Dogs do not think like humans, nor do humans think like dogs, though we try. Unfortunately, a dog is incapable of figuring out how humans think, so the responsibility falls on the owner to adopt a proper canine mindset. Dogs cannot rationalise, and dogs exist

DID YOU KNOW?
Dogs and humans may be the only animals that laugh. They imitate the smile on their owner's face when they greet each other. The dog only smiles at its human friends. It never smiles at another dog or cat. Usually it rolls up its lips and shows its teeth in a clenched mouth while it rolls over onto its back begging for a soft scratch.

in the present moment. Many dog owners make the mistake in training of thinking that they can reprimand their dog for something he did a while ago. Basically, you cannot even reprimand a dog for something he did 20 seconds ago! Either catch him in the act or forget it! It is a waste of your and your dog's time—in his mind, you are reprimanding him for whatever he is doing at that moment.

The following behavioural problems represent some which owners most commonly encounter. Every dog is unique and every situation is unique. No author could purport to solve your Cocker's problem simply by

The Cocker puppy in a warm, snugly lap is perfectly content. The other puppies want the same attention!

DID YOU KNOW?

Fear in a grown dog is often the result of improper or incomplete socialisation as a pup, or it can be the result of a traumatic experience he suffered when young. Keep in mind that the term 'traumatic' is relative—something that you would not think twice about can leave a lasting negative impression on a puppy. If the dog experiences a similar experience later in life, he may try to fight back to protect himself. Again, this behaviour is very unpredictable, especially if you do not know what is triggering his fear.

reading a script. Here we outline some basic 'dogspeak' so that owners' chances of solving behavioural problems are increased. Discuss bad habits with your veterinary surgeon and he/she can recommend a behavioural specialist to consult in appropriate cases. Since behavioural abnormalities are the leading reason owners abandon their pets, we hope that you will make a valiant effort to solve your Cocker's problem. Patience and understanding are virtues that dwell in every pet-loving household.

AGGRESSION

Although Cocker Spaniels are very gentle by nature, aggression can occur and then it is a problem. Aggressive behaviour is not to be tolerated. It is important to get to the root of the problem to ascertain why the dog is acting in this manner. Aggression is a display of dominance, and the dog should not have the dominant role in its pack, which is, in this case, your family. Have you been firm enough with the puppy or did you accept his dominant behaviour because it was so "cute"? Didn't you have time to go to the puppy classes and is this the price you have to pay?

The best solution is to consult a behavioural specialist, one who has experience with the Cocker Spaniel if possible. Together, perhaps you can pinpoint the cause of your dog's aggression and do something about it.

BEHAVIOUR TOWARD OTHER DOGS

If a dog is aggressive or fearful of another dog, this behaviour stems from not enough exposure to other dogs at an early age.

It is very important that a puppy learns to trust people and other dogs. When something or someone frightens him, many owners tend to react in a protective way. They pick the puppy up, comfort him and, thus, strengthen his belief that what happened was very scary indeed. If he gets frightened, do not pick him up; instead talk to him in a gentle but firm way and go on as if nothing happened. That way he will learn that indeed, nothing happened.

SEXUAL BEHAVIOUR

Dogs exhibit certain sexual behaviours that may have influenced your choice of male or female when you first purchased your Cocker Spaniel.

Female dogs usually have two oestruses per year, each season lasting about three weeks. These are the only times in which a female dog will mate, and she usually will not allow this until the second week of the cycle. If a bitch is not bred during the heat cycle,

DID YOU KNOW?

Males, whether whole or altered, will mount most anything: a pillow, your leg or, much to your horror, even your neighbour's leg. As with other types of inappropriate behaviour, the dog must be corrected while in the act, which for once is not difficult. Often he will not let go! While a puppy, experimenting with his very first urges, his owners feel he needs to 'sow his oats' and allow the pup to mount. As the pup grows into a full-size dog, with full-size urges, it becomes a nuisance and an embarrassment. Males always appear as if they are trying to 'save the race,' more determined and strong than imaginable. While altering the dog at an appropriate age will limit the dog's desire, it usually does not remove it entirely.

Friendship between Cockers can mimic human friendship. Some dogs are very good friends and protect each other. Other dogs can be very territorial and become aggressive when their leadership is challenged.

it is not uncommon for her to experience a false pregnancy, in which her mammary glands swell and she exhibits maternal tendencies toward toys or other objects.

Owners must further recognise that mounting is not merely a sexual expression but also one of dominance. Be consistent and persistent and you will find that you can 'move mounters.'

CHEWING

The national canine pastime is chewing! Every dog loves to sink his 'canines' into a tasty bone, but sometimes that bone is attached to his owner's hand! Dogs need to chew in order to massage their gums, to make their new teeth feel better and to exercise their jaws. This is a natural behaviour deeply imbedded in all things canine. Our role as owners is not to stop chewing but to redirect it to positive, chew-worthy objects. Be an informed owner and purchase proper chew toys for your

Cocker, like strong nylon bones made for large dogs. Be sure that the devices are safe and durable, since your dog's safety is at risk. Again, the owner is responsible for ensuring a dog-proof environment. The best answer is prevention: that is, put your shoes, handbags and other tasty objects in their proper places (out of the reach of the growing canine mouth). Direct puppies to their toys whenever you see them tasting the furniture legs or your trouser leg. Make a loud noise to attract the pup's attention and immediately escort him to his chew toy and engage him with the toy for at least four minutes, praising and encouraging him all the while.

Some trainers recommend deterrents, such as hot pepper or another bitter spice or a product designed for this purpose, to discourage the dog from chewing on unwanted objects. This is sometimes reliable, though not as often as the manufacturers of such products claim. Test out the product with your own dog before investing in a case of it.

JUMPING UP
Jumping up is a dog's friendly way of saying hello! Some dog owners do not mind when their dog jumps up, which is fine for them. The problem arises when guests come to the house and the dog greets them in the same manner—whether they like it or not! However friendly the greeting may be, chances are your visitors will not appreciate having two very muddy pawprints on their white clothes. The dog will not be able to distinguish upon whom he can jump and whom he cannot. Therefore, it is probably best to discourage this behaviour entirely.

Pick a command such as 'off' (avoid using 'down' since you will use that for the dog to lie down) and tell him 'off' when he jumps up. Place him on the ground on all fours and have him sit, praising him the whole time. Always lavish him with praise and petting when he is in the 'sit' position. That way you are still giving him a warm affectionate greeting because you are as excited to see him as he is to see you!

vide him with food and shelter, he has no need to use his paws for these purposes, and so the energy that he would be using manifests itself in the form of little holes all over your garden and flower beds.

Perhaps your dog is digging as a reaction to boredom—it is somewhat similar to someone eating a whole bag of pretzels in front of the telly—because they are there and there is not anything better to do! Basically, the answer is to provide the dog with adequate play

Many dog owners like their dogs to jump up upon them when they return home. Visitors may not welcome your Cocker's muddy-pawed greeting. Train the dog not to jump when it is a puppy.

DIGGING

Digging, which is seen as a destructive behaviour to humans, is actually quite a natural behaviour in dogs. Whether or not your dog is one of the 'earth dogs' (also known as terriers), his desire to dig can be irrepressible and most frustrating to his owners. When digging occurs in your garden, it is actually a normal behaviour redirected into something the dog can do in his everyday life. For example, in the wild a dog would be actively seeking food, making his own shelter, etc. He would be using his paws in a purposeful manner; he would be using them for his survival. Since you pro-

DID YOU KNOW?

When a dog bites there is always a reason for it doing so. Many dogs are trained to protect a person, an area or an object. When that person, area or object is violated the dog will attack. A dog attacks with its mouth. It has no other means of attack. It never uses teeth for defence. It merely runs away or lays down on the ground when it is in an indefensible situation. Fighting dogs (and there are many breeds which fight) are taught to fight, but they also have a natural instinct to fight. This instinct is normally reserved for other dogs, though unfortunate accidents occur when babies crawl towards a fighting dog and the dog mistakes the crawling child as a potential attacker.

If a dog is a biter for no reason; if it bites the hand that feeds it; if it snaps at members of your family. See your veterinarian immediately for behavioural modification treatments.

DID YOU KNOW?
Preventing bad behaviour before it happens is preferable to punishing a dog for misbehaving. Many common behaviour problems comes from a lack of proper training and the dog's not knowing what is expected of him. With training, most problems can be corrected. Disciplinary action on your part can do more harm than good.

and exercise so that his mind and paws are occupied, and so that he feels as if he is doing something useful.

Of course, digging is easiest to control if it is stopped as soon as possible, but it is often hard to catch a dog in the act, especially if he is alone in the garden during the day. If your dog is a compulsive digger and is not easily distracted by other activities, you can designate an area on your property where it is okay for him to dig. If you catch him digging in an off-limits area of the garden, immediately bring him to the approved area and praise him for digging there. Keep a close eye on him so that you can catch him, that is the only way he is going to understand what is permitted and what is not. If you bring him to a hole he dug an hour ago and tell him 'No,' he will understand that you are not fond of holes, or dirt, or flowers.

If you catch him while he is stifle-deep in your tulips, that is when he will get your message.

BARKING
Dogs cannot talk—oh, what they would say if they could! Instead, barking is a dog's way of 'talking.' It can be somewhat frustrating because it is not always easy to tell what a dog means by his bark—is he excited, happy, frightened, angry? Whatever it is that the dog is trying to say, he should not be punished for barking. It is only when the barking becomes excessive, and when the excessive barking becomes a bad habit, does the behaviour need to be modified. If an intruder came into your home in the middle of the night and the dog barked a warning, wouldn't you be pleased? You would probably deem your dog a hero, a wonderful guardian and protector of the home. On the other hand, if a friend drops by unexpectedly

DID YOU KNOW?
Your dog inherited the pack-leader mentality. He knows about pecking order and he instinctively wants to be top dog, but you have to convince him that you are the boss. There is no such thing as living in a democracy with your dog—you are the sole ruler!

DID YOU KNOW?

To encourage proper barking, you can teach your dog the command 'quiet.' When someone comes to the door and the dog barks a few times, praise him. Talk to him soothingly and when he stops barking, tell him 'quiet' and continue to praise him. In this sense you are letting him bark his warning, which is an instinctive behaviour, and then rewarding him for being quiet after a few barks. You may initially reward him with a treat after he has been quiet for a few minutes.

and rings the doorbell and is greeted with a sudden sharp bark, you would probably be annoyed at the dog. But isn't it just the same behaviour? The dog does not know any better…unless he sees who is at the door and it is someone he is familiar with, he will bark as a means of vocalising that his (and your) territory is being threatened. While your friend is not posing a threat, it is all the same to the dog. Barking is his means of letting you know that there is an intrusion, whether friend or foe, on your property. This type of barking is instinctive and should not be discouraged.

Excessive habitual barking, however, is a problem that should be corrected early on. As

your Cocker Spaniel grows up, you will be able to tell when his barking is purposeful and when it is for no reason. You will become able to distinguish your dog's different barks and with what they are associated. For example, the bark when someone comes to the door will be different from the bark when he is excited to see you. It is similar to a person's tone of voice, except that the dog has to rely totally on tone of voice because he does not have the benefit of using words. An incessant barker will be evident at an early age.

There are some things that encourage a dog to bark. For example, if your dog barks non-stop for a few minutes and you give him a treat to quieten him, he believes that you are rewarding him for barking. He will associate barking with getting a treat, and will keep doing it until he is rewarded.

DID YOU KNOW?

If your dog barks or growls at strangers for no reason, or if he growls when someone approaches him while he is eating, playing with a toy or taking a rest in a favourite spot, he is exhibiting territorial behaviour that could end in a display of aggression. This is potentially dangerous and may require the help of a behaviour specialist.

Rub any Cocker's tummy and watch him smile!

surprise the dog when he is looking for a mid-afternoon snack. Such remote-control devices, though not the first choice of some trainers, allow the correction to come from the object instead of the owner. These devices are also useful to keep the snacking hound from napping on furniture that is forbidden.

BEGGING

Just like food stealing, begging is a favourite pastime of hungry puppies! With that same reward—FOOD! Dogs quickly learn that their owners keep the 'good food' for themselves, and that we humans do not dine on dog biscuits. Begging is a conditioned response related to a specific stimulus, time and place. The sounds of the kitchen, cans and bottles opening, crinkling bags, the smell of food in preparation, etc., will excite the chow hound and soon the paws are in the air!

Here is the solution to stopping this behaviour: Never give into a beggar! You are rewarding the dog for sitting pretty, jumping up, whining and rubbing his nose into you

FOOD STEALING

Is your dog devising ways of stealing food from your counter tops? If so, you must answer the following questions: Is your Cocker hungry, or is he 'constantly famished' like every other chow hound? Why is there food on the counter top? Face it, some dogs are more food-motivated than others; some dogs are totally obsessed by a slab of brisket and can only think of their next meal. Food stealing is terrific fun and always yields a great reward—FOOD, glorious food.

The owner's goal, therefore, is to make the 'reward' less rewarding, even startling! Plant a shaker can (an empty pop can with coins inside) on the counter so that it catches your pooch off guard. There are other devices available that will

> ### DID YOU KNOW?
> Never scream, shout, jump or run about if you want your dog to stay calm. You set the example for your dog's behaviour in most circumstances. Learn from your dog's reaction to your behaviour and act accordingly.

by giving him that glorious reward—food. By ignoring the dog, you will (eventually) force the behaviour into extinction. Note that the behaviour likely gets worse before it disappears, so be sure there are not any 'softies' in the family who will give in to little 'Oliver' every time he whimpers, 'More, please.'

SEPARATION ANXIETY
Your Cocker Spaniel may howl, whine or otherwise vocalise his displeasure at your leaving the house and his being left alone. This is a normal case of separation anxiety, but there are things that can be done to eliminate this problem. Your dog needs to learn that he will be fine on his own for a while and that he will not wither away if he is not

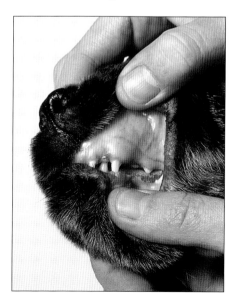

All puppies are prone to separation anxiety. Cockers that usually come from large litters have their siblings and dam for company before they go to new owners. A single-puppy home is a huge adjustment.

attended to every minute of the day. In fact, constant attention can lead to separation anxiety in the first place. If you are endlessly coddling and cooing over your dog, he will come to expect this from you all of the time and it will be more traumatic for him when you are not there. Obviously, you enjoy spending time with your dog, and he thrives on your love and attention. However, it should not

A dog does not have to be large to cause harm with its bite. Undisciplined and unruly dogs can become aggressive and dangerous in the hands of irresponsible owners.

DID YOU KNOW?
Barking is your dog's way of protecting you. If he barks at a stranger walking past your house, a moving car or a fleeing cat, he is merely exercising his responsibility to protect his pack (YOU) and territory from a perceived intruder. Since the 'intruder' usually keeps going, the dog thinks his barking chased it away and he feels fulfilled. Barking of this type is a normal response; excessive barking for no reason should be discouraged.

DID YOU KNOW?

Dogs left alone for a length of time may react wildly when you return. Sometimes they run, jump, bite, chew, tear things apart, wet themselves or behave in a very undisciplined manner. Allow them to calm down before greeting them or they will consider your attention as a reward for their antics.

your dog starts whimpering as you approach the door, your first instinct will be to run to him and comfort him, but do not do it! Really—eventually he will adjust and be just fine if you take it in small steps. His anxiety stems from being placed in an unfamiliar situation; by familiarising him with being alone he will learn that he is okay. That is not to say you should purposely leave your dog home alone, but the dog needs to know that while he can depend on you for his care, you do not have to be by his side 24 hours a day.

When the dog is alone in the house, he should be confined to his crate or a designated

become a dependent relationship where he is heartbroken without you.

One thing you can do to minimise separation anxiety is to make your entrances and exits as low-key as possible. Do not give your dog a long drawn-out goodbye, and do not lavish him with hugs and kisses when you return. This is giving in to the attention that he craves, and it will only make him miss it more when you are away. Another thing you can try is to give your dog a treat when you leave; this will not only keep him occupied and keep his mind off the fact that you just left, but it will also help him associate your leaving with a pleasant experience.

You may have to accustom your dog to being left alone in small increments, much like when you introduced your pup to his crate. Of course, when

DID YOU KNOW?

The number of dogs who suffer from separation anxiety is on the rise as more and more pet owners find themselves at work all day. New attention is being paid to this problem, which is especially hard to diagnose since it is only evident when the dog is alone. Research is currently being done to help educate dog owners about separation anxiety and about how they can help minimise this problem in their dogs.

dog-proof area of the house. This should be the area in which he sleeps, so he should already feel comfortable there and this should make him feel more at ease when he is alone. This is just one of the many examples in which a crate is an invaluable tool for you and your dog, and another reinforcement of why your dog should view his crate as a 'happy' place, a place of his own.

COPROPHAGIA

Faeces eating is, to most humans, one of the most disgusting behaviours that their dog could engage in, yet to the dog it is perfectly normal. It is hard for us to understand why a dog would want to eat its own faeces; he could be seeking certain nutrients that are missing from his diet, he could be just plain hungry, or he could be attracted by the pleasing (to a dog) scent. While coprophagia most often refers to the dog eating his own faeces, a dog may likely eat that of another animal as well if he comes across it. Vets have found that diets with a low digestibility, containing relatively

> **DID YOU KNOW?**
> Owners who adopt an adult dog with a history of aggression must be prepared to deal with the situation. The dog will usually be more aggressive in a new home where his leadership is unchallenged and unquestioned (in his mind).

low levels of fibre and high levels of starch, increase coprophagia. Therefore, high-fibre diets may decrease the likelihood of dogs eating faeces. Both the consistency of the stool (how firm it feels in the dog's mouth) and the presence of undigested nutrients increase the likelihood. Dogs often find the stool of cats and horses more palatable than that of other dogs. Once the dog develops diarrhoea from faeces eating, it will likely quit this distasteful habit, since dogs tend to prefer eating harder faeces.

Young Cockers often outgrow coprophagia, but a clean garden will prevent your pup from indulging in this bad habit altogether.

167

DID YOU KNOW?

If you are approached by an aggressive, growling dog, do not run away. Simply stand still and avoid eye contact. If you have something in your hand (like a handbag), throw it sideways away from your body to distract the dog from making a frontal attack.

DID YOU KNOW?

DANGER! If you and your on-lead dog are approached by a dog that is not restrained, walk away from the dog as quickly as possible. Don't allow your dog to make eye contact with the other dog. You should not make eye contact either. In dog terms, eye contact indicates a challenge.

To discourage this behaviour, first make sure that the food you are feeding your dog is nutritionally complete and that he is getting enough food. If changes in his diet do not seem to work, and no medical cause can be found, you will have to modify the behaviour through environmental control before it becomes a habit. There are some tricks you can try, such as adding an unpleasant-tasting substance to the faeces to make them unpalatable or adding something to the dog's food which will make it unpleasant tasting after it passes through the dog. The best way to prevent your dog from eating his stool is to make it unavailable— clean up after he eliminates and remove any stool from the garden. If it is not there, he cannot eat it.

Never reprimand the dog for stool eating, as this rarely impresses the dog. Vets recommend distracting the dog while he is in the act of stool eating. Another option is to muzzle the dog when he is in the garden to relieve himself; this usually is effective within 30 to 60 days. Coprophagia most frequently is seen in pups 6 to 12 months of age, and usually disappears around the dog's first birthday..

Sometimes dogs that are restrained in small quarters eat faeces to keep themselves clean. Your Cocker should always have the opportunity to relieve himself in the appropriate place so that this will not be an issue.

168

How impression-
able and pre-
cious are young
Cocker puppies?
Adopting a
Cocker into your
family is a seri-
ous undertaking.
You owe it to
your new trust-
ing puppy to
provide him with
the very best for
his whole life.

GLOSSARY

This glossary is intended to help you, the Cocker Spaniel owner, better understand the specific terms used in this book as well as other terms that might surface in discussions with your veterinary surgeon during his care of your Cocker Spaniel.

Abscess a pus-filled inflamed area of body tissue.

Acral lick granuloma unexplained licking of an area, usually the leg, that prevents healing of original wound.

Acute disease a disease whose onset is sudden and fast.

Albino an animal totally lacking in pigment (always white).

Allergy a known sensitivity that results from exposure to a given allergen.

Alopecia lack of hair.

Amaurosis an unexplained blindness from the retina.

Anaemia red-blood-cell deficiency.

Arthritis joint inflammation.

Atopic dermatitis congenital-allergen-caused inflammation of the skin.

Atrophy wasting away caused by faulty nutrition; a reduction in size.

Bloat gastric dilatation.

Calculi mineral 'stone' located in a vital organ, i.e., gall bladder.

Cancer a tumour that continues to expand and grow rapidly.

Carcinoma cancerous growth in the skin.

Cardiac arrhythmia irregular heartbeat.

Cardiomyopathy heart condition involving the septum and flow of blood.

Cartilage strong but pliable body tissue.

Cataract clouding of the eye lens.

Cherry eye third eyelid prolapsed gland.

Cleft palate improper growth of the two hard palates of the mouth.

Collie eye anomaly congenital defect of the back of the eye.

Congenital not the same as hereditary, but present at birth.

Congestive heart failure fluid buildup in lungs due to heart's inability to pump.

Conjunctivitis inflammation of the membrane that lines eyelids and eyeball.

Cow hocks poor rear legs that point inward; always incorrect.

Cryptorchid male animal with only one or both testicles undescended.

Cushing's disease condition caused by adrenal gland producing too much corticosteroid.

Cyst uninflamed swelling contain non-pus-like fluid.

Degeneration deterioration of tissue.

Demodectic mange red-mite infestation caused by *Demodex canis.*

Dermatitis skin inflammation.

Dew claw a functionless digit found on the inside of a dog's leg.

Diabetes insipidus disease of the hypothalamus gland resulting in animal passing great amounts of diluted urine.

Diabetes mellitus excess of glucose in blood stream.

Distemper contagious viral disease of dogs that can be most deadly.

Distichiasis double layer of eyelashes on an eyelid.

Dysplasia abnormal, poor development of a body part, especially a joint.

Dystrophy inherited degeneration.

Eclampsia potentially deadly disease in post-partum bitches due to calcium deficiency.

Ectropion outward turning of the eyelid; opposite of entropion.

Eczema inflammatory skin disease, marked by itching.

Entropion inward turning of the eyelid.

Epilepsy chronic disease of the nervous system characterised by seizures.

Exocrine pancreatic insufficiency body's inability to produce enough enzymes to aid digestion.

False pregnancy pseudo-pregnancy, bitch shows all signs of pregnancy but there is no fertilisation.

Follicular mange demodectic mange.

Gastric dilatation bloat caused by the dog's swallowing air resulting in distended, twisted stomach.

Gastroenteritis stomach or intestinal inflammation.

Gingivitis gum inflammation caused by plaque buildup.

Glaucoma increased eye pressure affecting vision.

Haematemesis vomiting blood.

Haematoma blood-filled swollen area.

Haematuria blood in urine.

Haemophilia bleeding disorder due to lack of clotting factor.

Haemorrhage bleeding.

Heat stroke condition due to over-heating of an animal.

Heritable an inherited condition.

Hot spot moist eczema characterised by dog's licking in same area.

Hyperglycaemia excess glucose in blood.

Hypersensitivity allergy.

Hypertrophic cardiomyopathy left-ventricle septum becomes thickened and obstructs blood flow to heart.

Hypertrophic osteodystrophy condition affecting normal bone development.

Hypothyroidism disease caused by insufficient thyroid hormone.

Hypertrophy increased cell size resulting in enlargement of organ.

Hypoglycaemia glucose deficiency in blood.

Idiopathic disease of unknown cause.

IgA deficiency immunoglobin deficiency resulting in digestive, breathing and skin problems.

Inbreeding mating two closely related animals, eg, mother—son.

Inflammation the changes that occur to a tissue after injury, characterised by swelling, redness, pain, etc.

Jaundice yellow colouration of mucous membranes.

Keratoconjunctivitis sicca dry eye.

Leukaemia malignant disease characterised by white blood cells released into blood stream.

Lick granuloma excessive licking of a wound, preventing proper healing.

Merle coat colour that is diluted.

Monorchid a male animal with only one testicle descended.

Neuritis nerve inflammation.

Nicitating membrane third eyelid pulling across the eye.

Nodular dermatofibrosis lumps on toes and legs, usually associated with cancer of kidney and uterus.

Oedema fluid accumulation in a specific area.

Osteochondritis bone or cartilage inflammation.

Outcrossing mating two breed representatives from different families.

Pancreatitis pancreas inflammation.

Pannus chronic superficial keratitis, affecting pigment and blood vessels of cornea.

Panosteitis inflammation of leg bones, characterised by lameness.

Papilloma wart.

Patellar luxation slipped kneecap, common in small dogs.

Patent ductus arteriosus an open blood vessel between pulmonary artery and aorta.

Penetrance frequency in which a trait shows up in offspring of animals carrying that inheritable trait.

Periodontitis acute or chronic inflammation of tissue surround the tooth.

Pneumonia lung inflammation.

Progressive retinal atrophy congenital disease of retina causing blindness.

Pruritis persistent itching.

Retinal atrophy thin retina.

Seborrhea dry scurf or excess oil deposits on the skin.

Stomatitis mouth inflammation.

Tumour solid or fluid-filled swelling resulting from abnormal growth.

Uremia waste product buildup in blood due to disease of kidneys.

Uveitis inflammation of the iris.

Von Willebrand's disease hereditary bleeding disease.

Wall eye lack of colour in the iris.

Weaning separating the mother from her dependent, nursing young.

Zoonosis animal disease communicable to humans.

Acrodermatitis 119
Adult diet 72
Ageing signs 143
Aggression 158
Agility 109, 150-151
America 22
American Kennel Club 24
—address 152
Ancylostoma caninum **133-134**
Ascaris lumbricoides **133, 135**
Axelrod, Dr. Herbert R. 131
Backpacking 109
Barking 162
Basic commands 99
Bathing 80
Bedding 55
Begging 164
Ben Bowdler 15
Bentley, Patricia 18
Berners, Juliana 11
Black 30
Black-and-white 33
Blue Peter 16
Blue roan 33
Boarding 84
Bones 56, 160
Bowls 58
Breaside Bustle 15
Breed club 48
Breed split 24
Breeders 28, 45, 47
British Veterinary Association 136
Brushing 76
Burial 142
Buying your puppy 50
Caddy, Joyce 18
Caius 11
Canadian Kennel Club
—address 152
Caniou Cambrai 18
Canis domesticus 12
Canterbury Tales 10
Cat flea 127
Cataracts 116, 138
Challenge Certificates 147
Championship Shows 148

Chaucer, Geoffrey 10
Chewing 56, 70, 94, 159
Cheyletiella 131
Chloe II 22
Choosing 45
Coat 29
Cocker Spaniel Club of Great
Britain 14
Collar 58, 98
Collins, A.W. 20
Colour 29-30, 46
Come 103
Coronavirus 120
Cox, Nicolas 13
Crate 53, 83, 91
Crate training 55, 92
Crying 69
Ctenocephalides canis **127**
Ctenocephalides felis **127**
Cypriote collection 9
De Casembroot, Judy 16
Demodex 131
Dental examination 113
Dermacentor variabilis **129-130**
Development schedule 93
Digging 161
Dirofilaria immitis **137**
Discipline 96
Distemper 120
Dodge, Geraldine R. 24
Dog flea 127
Dog tick 129-130
Down 100
Doxford, Kay 17
Dry bath 81
Ear cleaning 81
Ear mites 131
Echinococcus multilocularis 134
Europe 21
Euthanasia 141
Exemption shows 148
Exercise 75
Exquisite Model of Ware 17
Exquisite of Ware 15
External parasites 123
Faeces eating 167

Familial nephropathy (FN) 116, 136
Family introduction 62
Farrow, James 14
Fédération Cynologique
Internationale 37, 136, 153
—address 152
Feeding 71
—adults 72
—puppy 71
—seniors 73
Fence 61
Field Spaniel 13, 22
Field trials 152
First aid 117
Fleas 123, 132
Fletcher, F.F. 22
Flush 9
Food allergies 122
Food intolerance 123
Food reward 106
Food stealing 164
Gaston the Foix 10
Germany 24
Gold, A.H. 16
Good Citizen Dog award 151
Gundog training 107
Heartworm 134, 137
Heel 104
Henry IV 11
Hepatitis 120
Hereditary defects 48
Hip dysplasia 136
Holland 24
Holmes, Kay 18
Home preparation 52
Hookworm 133-134
Hot spots 119
House-training 75, 89
Howe, Lorna Countess 17
Howell Dha 10
Identification 85
Internal organs 110
Internal parasites 131
Invader of Ware 15
Ixode **131**
Jones, Sylvia 18

Jumping up 160
Kennel Club, The 37, 50, 136, 146
  —address 152
Kennel cough 120
Keyes, John 11
Lead 57, 98
Leader 66
Leptospirosis 120
Lice 129
Life span 139
Liver 30
Livre de Chasse 10
Lloyd, H.S. 15, 21
Lloyd, R. 15
Lochranza 18
Lucas-Lucas, Veronica 17
Lucky Star of Ware 17
Lupus 119
Lyme disease 130
Mange 131
Metropolitan Museum 9
Microchip implantation 86
Miroir de Phoebus 10
Mites 130
Mosquitoes 135
Nail clipping 82
Newspaper 90
Nipping 68
Nose 108
Obo 14
Obo II 22
Of Ware 15
Open Shows 148
Ouaine Chieftain 18
Parasite bites 118
Parasites 123, 131
Parasiticides 129
Parti-colours 32
Parvovirus 120
Pedigree 50
Peele, R. de D. 15
Personality 27
Porter, J.M. 16
Prince Henry 11
Progressive retinal atrophy (PRA) 138
Psoroptes bovis **132**
Punishment 97

Puppy diet 71
Puppy problems 68
Puppy training 88
Puppy-proofing 60
Rabies 120
Registration papers 50
Reward 97
Rhabditis **134**
Rhipicephalus sanguineus **131**
Roan 32
Robinson, Mollie 20
Rocky Mountain spotted fever 130
Roundworms 132-133, 135
Sable-and-white 30
Scabies 131
Schofield, Dilys 21
Selection 45
Senior diet 73
Separation anxiety 165
Sex 45
Sexual behaviour 159
Sit 99
Socialisation 65
Solid 32
Spain 9
Sporting Spaniel Society 23
Sportsman's Cabinet 13, 30
Standard 14, 37, 149
Stay 102

Tan markings 32
Tapeworms 133
Tattooing 86
Temperament 28, 47
Thorndike's Theory of Learning 97
Ticking 32
Ticks 130
Toxocara canis 132
Toys 55
Tracy Witch of Ware 17
Travelling with your dog 83
Treatise of Dogges 30
Treatise of Englishe Dogges 11
Treats 98, 106
Tri-colour 33
Trimming 77
Vaccination schedule 114
Van Herwaarden, L. 21
Veterinary surgeon 111
Water 75
Whining 69
Whoopee of Ware 15
Wiley, J.P. 22
Woodcock's Memory's 22
Woolf, Virginia 9
Woolf, Mrs. 20
Working tests 152
Working trials 151
World War II 18

My Cocker Spaniel

PUT YOUR PUPPY'S FIRST PICTURE HERE

Dog's Name _____

Date _____ Photographer _____